T0328741

VICTORIAN FICTION

An Exhibition of Original Editions
at 7 Albemarle Street, London
January to February 1947
arranged by

JOHN CARTER

with the collaboration of

MICHAEL SADLEIR

PUBLISHED FOR
THE NATIONAL BOOK LEAGUE
BY THE
CAMBRIDGE UNIVERSITY PRESS
1947

CAMBRIDGE
UNIVERSITY PRESS

University Printing House, Cambridge CB2 8BS, United Kingdom

Cambridge University Press is part of the University of Cambridge.

It furthers the University's mission by disseminating knowledge in the pursuit of
education, learning and research at the highest international levels of excellence.

www.cambridge.org
Information on this title: www.cambridge.org/9781107536791

© Cambridge University Press 1947

First published 1947
First paperback edition 2015

A catalogue record for this publication is available from the British Library

ISBN 978-1-107-53679-1 Paperback

CONTENTS OF THE CATALOGUE

FOREWORD

By Michael Sadleir

This exhibition—both externally and internally—may fairly be termed spectacular. As Mr Carter explains in his Introduction, the period covered (1837–1901) witnessed, in book-design and manufacture, the displacement of the pallid dignity of semi-permanent boards with paper spine-labels by brightly coloured cloths and lavish use of gold. Further, it saw the invention of woodblock printing in colours, which led to increasingly elaborate experiment with book-covers and book-illustrations. In consequence, as no one can deny, the exhibits add up to a colourful, vigorous and decorative ensemble.

In the second place (and on this also Mr Carter lays stress) only very few of the visitors to the exhibition will have had a previous opportunity of seeing what Victorian published fiction really looked like when it was new. Books of the board, board-half-cloth and cloth periods (the last-named especially) are nowadays virtually impossible to find in impeccable original condition. The organizers are fully aware that they have included in their show certain titles not in that condition. This they were driven to do because nothing better could be found. On the other hand, the number which (in the jargon of the craft of collecting) are called 'mint' or 'very fine' copies, is indeed phenomenal; and the sight of these as they appeared in the bookshops on publication will, it is hoped, cause many spectators to revise their opinion as to Victorian taste in decoration.

It will be noted that liking for ornament plots a rising curve from the sixties to the late eighties (a gentle one from the forties to about 1860, followed for another twenty years by unashamed exuberance) and then falls steeply, through a brief epoch of effeminate prettiness, to the comparative austerity of the one-volume novel. Publishers and binders had a gay time while the three-decker lasted; but a drop from a published price of anything from twenty shillings to thirty-one-and-six to a flat nominal six shillings (less trade discount, actually four-and-sixpence) meant counting pence where before one hardly counted shillings. At the time the new simplicity was thought very elegant, and the legend of Victorian ugliness was born. Bibliophiles of to-day, too often condemned to thin drab paper, grey ink, mean strawboards and cloth lacking quality and variety, may feel as nostalgic for opulent and glossy bookmaking as for the châteaubriand and fried potatoes, which in younger, braver days we fearlessly demolished.

In the third place the exhibition offers, in terms of novel-writing, a panorama of a period in British history when perhaps more mental activity existed than ever before, when social contrasts were more violent, snobbery more widespread, dutiful well-doing more determined and self-effacing. All these—and twenty other aspects of the life and aspirations, the hypocrisies and the idealisms, the abnegations and the materialisms of Victorian England—find expression in the stories displayed and classified. There are great books among them, and books which, as literature, deserve to be forgotten; but there is not one which does not in some way tell—and from first-hand knowledge—of the pleasures, hardships, charity, selfishness, spiritual unease and complacency, of the long reign which enthroned our country, whether for good or ill, as seemingly the most powerful and established in the world.

Victoria's sixty years were not, as is sometimes assumed, a period of unbroken and prosperous calm. Her first decade, culminating in the European convulsions of 1848, saw the country nearer to social disaster than ever before. It was saved by the joint disciplinary action of Evangelicanism and Utilitarianism—the two often in conflict, yet at one in upholding a moral stability based respectively on zeal for holiness and faith in reason. Various elements in this period of tension are here presented in novel form. The social revelations of Dickens and Mrs Gaskell, the constructive compromises of Disraeli and Charles Kingsley, the witty epitaphs of Mrs Gore on the grave of the tinsel aristocracy of the thirties—these reflect the turmoil and the sense of shifting foundations which, about 1850, suddenly jarred the solvent middle-classes to an awareness of the dreadful conditions of slum-life and the threat implicit in an underworld of poverty, dwelling in degradation and breeding recklessly. The fifties show this social consciousness at work; and the emergence, as dominant influence in the country and therefore as favourite theme of fiction, of a dutiful prudish *bourgeoisie*, taking its cue from a virtuous court surrounding a virtuous queen. Religious controversy now becomes an absorbing interest, to which during the sixties is added political theorizing and discussion of the ethics and systems of education. With the late seventies the intrusion into good society of stock gambling and company promotion marked the economic and, in consequence, social weakening of the aristocrats and gentlefolk, to whom personal integrity and duty towards their neighbours had been implicit in their caste. It was the first flush of imperialism, which foretold a mounting fever and the squalid tragedy of the South African War.

All the time the national genius for sport and sea-faring produces its own literature; the taste for sensation-fiction recreates the gothic romance in terms of Victorianism; and, most prolific of all, the novelists of social manners (among whom we now recognize Trollope as supreme) devise their infinite variations of polite love-making, tuft-hunting and pleasant domesticity.

So we come to the nineties and the final decade of our allotted period. It is tempting to take this epoch at one of its three face-values—as the climax of national power, permanence and peace of mind; or as an almost too perfect sunlit serenity, a 'weather breeder' which preceded a time of storms; or as witnessing the acceptance by literature and painting of the doctrine of Art for Art's Sake. Rightly we must regard all three; and to that end appropriate novels are provided.

Let this brief summary of the purpose and significance of our exhibition conclude with a quotation from George Sampson's *Concise Cambridge History of English Literature*, which admirably presents the British scene at the moment when we take leave of it.

Only those who were adult observers of life in the last dozen years of the nineteenth century can know the thrill and exaltation of that time. The country had Security. Science had shaken the foundations of biblical theology, but the foundations of religion stood fast; and those who had abandoned the traditional creeds, had not abandoned their belief in the permanence of moral order in the world....Great Britain was indisputably the first of nations, and her Navy kept ceaseless watch on the Seven Seas. The Diamond Jubilee of Queen Victoria seemed such a natural demonstration of lasting security, that the *Recessional* of Kipling appeared to sound a note of warning almost untimely in its seriousness.

But already there was a cloud in the summer sky. The great Dock Strike of 1889 had changed for ever the relations between employers and employed.... Far away in South Africa affairs were going ill....At the end of 1895 came the ignominious Jameson raid; in 1899 war was declared against the Boers....The war left England without a friend in the world...the might of Britain, impressively exhibited at the Jubilee, had proved to be almost ridiculously vulnerable, and the traditional calm of the English descended without shame to the hysterics of 'mafficking'.

Finally a few sentences about Literature:

Literature, in the narrowest sense, had stood aloof from all causes other than the artistic. The writers of the 'nineties were much concerned with 'style', and the 'right word' and the 'authentic note'—with rhythm and significance and values....But it is an easy mistake to suppose that the literature of the last Victorian decade was a literature of decadence....Ernest Dowson was a poet of the 'nineties; but so was Rudyard Kipling. *The Picture of Dorian Gray* was a novel of the 'nineties; but so was *The Time Machine*. Hubert Crackanthorpe was an essayist of the 'nineties; but so was George Bernard Shaw.

The view of the last decade of the nineteenth and the first decade of the twentieth as a period of florid opulence, luxuriating in traditionalism till awakened to realities by the rude shock of war, is ludicrously unlike the facts.... In tales, in poems and in essays, new themes and new styles were apparent. The shape of things to come was already foreshadowed.

INTRODUCTION TO THE EXHIBITION

By John Carter

Literature as a constituent in the life of a people is something more than the words put together by writers. The student of the literature of any kind or period—in our case the fiction of the Victorian age—has to take account of printers, binders, publishers, booksellers, lending libraries and last but not least readers. It has therefore been our objective in this exhibition not to present a mere list, in the form of books, of the two hundred or three hundred 'best' or 'greatest' or 'most popular' pieces of Victorian fiction, but to give, in addition to an inevitably fore-shortened survey of a great and a prolific period of novel *writing*, some idea of the reading habits of the public, the various methods by which fiction was produced and distributed, and what the results looked like as they were handed out across the bookshop or bookstall or lending-library counter.

The ordinary reader of Victorian fiction to-day knows his favourites either in a modern reprint or in some earlier edition, probably well thumbed and usually rebound, inherited from his youth or his parents. The curious may have satisfied a feeling for the fitness of form to matter by the acquisition of a contemporary or even an original edition. But very few except serious collectors of Victorian novels have any clear idea of what they looked like, individually, let alone collectively, when they were new. For though our period ended less than fifty years ago, the circumstances of its fiction publishing and fiction reading were such as to impose very heavy odds against the survival in good original condition of more than a fraction of the enormous output. It is easier to-day to find a well-preserved copy of Fielding's *Amelia* in original calf than of Thackeray's *Esmond* in original cloth: yet the former is a hundred years older.

That it has been possible to show here a representative selection from that output not only in its originally published form but, also important for our purpose, almost all of it in a brilliant state of preservation, is due to the devotion and discriminating skill of a single collector, Mr Michael Sadleir, whose unrivalled library has provided all but a handful of the material on display. Only fellow-specialists, perhaps, will fully appreciate the exceptional character of this assemblage and the extreme rarity of many of the books in such condition. But this is not an exhibition for specialists; it is designed as an eye-opener for that great majority of us who perforce think of Victorian fiction as originally published, if we think of it at all, in terms of half calf, shabby library copies of three-deckers, and tattered yellow-backs, because that is the way we normally encounter it. How different was the reality may be seen here.

The poor chances of survival in pristine state of the novels of the last century are due to the methods by which they were distributed. Most Victorian novels continued until near the end to be published in three (less often two) volumes: and the three-decker, which cost 31*s*. 6*d*., was meant to be borrowed from the library, not bought. The economic strangle-hold exerted on the fiction market by the lending libraries was, indeed, the legacy of an earlier era; but if it was more insolently flaunted in the Victorian period than ever before or since, it was not so much enforced as natural to a society in which book buying has always, alas, been confined to a few. That the attempts made by several mid-century publishers to break it by reducing the price of new novels were unsuccessful was primarily due to this inertia in the public: combined, however, with the loss of revenue to the author caused by the libraries' boycott and reduced royalties, which in turn drove the price-breakers to inferior writers, translations, etc.

The novels of fashionable 'society' in the thirties to fifties—the 'silver fork' school—which were bought in fair numbers by fashionable society itself, do, it is true, survive with comparative (though only comparative) frequency in original state. At any date, the author of course gave away a few copies, and his more devoted friends bought a few more. Unsuccessful titles might be sold off and survive in presentable shape (George Eliot's *Felix Holt* and Thackeray's *Philip* are examples familiar to the experts). But in the main, the circulating library was the grave of the three-decker as a physical specimen: for in the boards-and-label period, and in the half-cloth period (*ob.* late fifties), it would be rebound or leather-backed; and in the cloth period it would be disfigured by labels. Moreover, even those copies which were bought outright were apt to be rebound by their owners during the first half of the century, while at all times more people are Johnsons or Lambs than are studious to preserve immaculate what are, after all, things of use. Small wonder, then, that three- or two- (or even one-) volume novels of the Victorian age seldom survive to-day in anything approaching the condition in which they were born.

The one substantial challenge to the three-decker tradition, until in the eighties it began to totter under its own weight, was offered by the 'part-issue'. And it was in the very first year of Queen Victoria's reign that a successful marriage was consummated between the two different types of part-issue inherited from the previous century—the expensive picture book (with subsidiary text) for the drawing-room table, and the crude, cheap reissue, whether of entertainment or moral instruction, for the servant's hall and the school-room. For with the resounding success of *Pickwick*, publishers perceived that the public would spend their guinea or more to buy (not borrow) a novel by a popular author, almost always with plates by a popular illustrator, it if were issued on a sort of instalment system, in parts, at a shilling a month. The part-issue was chiefly suitable for established authors,[1] since it would only pay if the printing could be a large one; but many of the novels of Dickens, Thackeray, Trollope, Lever, Ainsworth and other 'best-selling' writers were issued in this form before, in the seventies, it lost its last battle against the magazine serial.

Yet the odds against the survival in decent order of part-issued books are not in fact much shorter than with three-deckers. For it was the normal usage to bind up the paper-wrappered series when complete, whether in half or full leather or in the cloth case provided by the publisher for the purpose. Consequently, sets of 'original parts', which like boarded novels (or French fiction to-day) were only half dressed until more solidly bound, have survived intact only by accident. As for the cloth-bound volumes (whether one or two) in which these books were also published at or near the end of the issue of parts, the substantial number of pages plus the heavy plate paper of the illustrations were too often too much for the shapely survival of their containing cloth.

It must not be supposed that because the Victorians mostly borrowed new novels they did not also buy fiction they had decided to like, and in very large numbers. The fiction reprint series was a powerful factor in Victorian publishing, and examples of several of the principal series are shown here. In addition, most novels which had had some success but were not included in a series achieved independent republication, just as they do to-day; usually at 6s. and after a very short interval; with the 'yellow-back', usually at 2s., as the contemporary equivalent of the wrappered 6d. or 1s. reprint of the thirties, for the longer-lived titles.

The last decade of the century saw the decline and disappearance (save for a few freak examples) of the three-decker. With the increase of the reading public and the proof that new novels at 6s. (or 4s. 6d. cash) would be bought in sufficient numbers to show author and publisher a profit, the grip of the lending libraries and their insistence on three-volume format relaxed.[2] Most of the novels of the nineties,

---

[1] Exceptions were made in favour of such comic or satirical works as *Valentine Vox*, *Sylvester Sound* or *Christopher Tadpole*, which depended heavily on their illustrators.

[2] This insistence was usually based on the argument that their subscribers were accustomed to value (i.e. bulk) for money; but it was reinforced by an ingenious method by which the customer was induced to subscribe for a minimum of three volumes at a time.

therefore, differ in appearance from those of the twenties and thirties only by virtue of their more individual, though hardly more elaborate, bindings. As for their contents, the relief from Procrustes' bed rapidly produced very salutary results. Many a novelist who had had to 'pad' to fill three volumes, however thinly spread on the page, found his true form in the unhampered elasticity of the 6*s*. format.

SCOPE AND ARRANGEMENT OF THE EXHIBITION

The strict confines of our period are 1837–1901; and it should be explained that just as we have excluded authors like Peacock, whose main but not complete output precedes the former date, so we have also excluded such authors as Galsworthy, Bennett and Conrad whose earliest novels precede the latter but whose *floruit* lies definitely in the present century.

Short stories have of course been admitted; but except for such writers as Kipling, who chiefly worked in this medium, they have normally yielded place to their authors' full-length works. Children's books as such have been avoided, since the *genus* has recently been exhaustively shown here. But the border line between books for boys and books for children is always a debatable one and we have not scrupled to trespass where the design of the exhibition called for it: as may be noticed particularly in the sections devoted to 'Adventure Stories' and 'Tales of the Sea', which (naturally, in view of our nautical tradition) themselves include some potentially interchangeable titles.

The exhibition is divided into two parts: the first functional, the second categorical. Sections A–H have been arranged to show what Victorian fiction looked like and how it was published, the examples being chosen primarily for their aptness as physical specimens and only secondarily for the interest of their contents. Sections J to the end are based on literary and historical criteria.

The latter half of the exhibition has been subdivided by subject, in order to show not only the diversity of Victorian fiction but also the strongly marked tradition found in certain categories. Yet a handful of the most important writers, though they will also be found represented in the subject-sections, clearly overtop any such categorization, and the first section (J) is accordingly devoted to 'The Giants'. Here the selection, both of the writers and the books, was undertaken with special diffidence, for it was bound to be based on the literary judgement of the organizers, with which many good judges will no doubt disagree. It is hoped, however, that the substantial representation accorded elsewhere in the exhibition to the half-dozen 'runners-up' will at least dispel any suggestions of disrespect.

Introduction to the Exhibition

DISPLAY AND CATALOGUE TECHNIQUE

The typography of novels during our period, mainly undistinguished, exhibits so few developments of any interest by comparison with the constant and significant changes in their exterior dress that almost all the books are shown as they would be seen on table, bookshop counter or shelf—i.e. not open but closed. Minor exceptions are due to the occasional[1] presence of author's inscriptions, as in the case of the two books presented by their authors to Queen Victoria and now graciously lent by H.M. The King. The major exception is the section devoted to illustrators, whose work is also shown round the walls.

The catalogue descriptions have been stripped of all irrelevant bibliographical detail. Though notes to individual books seemed necessary, and may be found useful, in the functional sections, any profusion of literary comment would be impertinent in so well known a field; and beyond the brief introductory notes to the subject-sections and some comments in Sections V and W it has been generally eschewed.

No rigid consistency has been observed in the treatment of authors' names, since our objective has been ready identification without fuss. Mrs Gaskell, for instance, is normally so called, so her 'Elizabeth Cleghorn' has been omitted; while less well-known writers are described either in full or by the style used on their own title-pages. Since the writing of fiction continued, well into our period, to be regarded by genteel persons as a frivolous, if not actually a degraded, occupation, many of the earlier novels shown were published either anonymously or as 'by the author of such-and-such': but their names have here been denuded, for simplicity's sake, of the customary square brackets. Pseudonyms are followed by '(=*real name*)': authors who, by marriage for instance, wrote under, or are known by, two names have the less familiar added in brackets.

Similarly, well known publishers like Longmans or Blackwood are given without trimmings and only the obscurer ones (e.g. John W. Parker) in full. London should be assumed in all imprints unless some other place is given. Sizes have been omitted altogether, since the visitor can see for himself, and will care little to be told which is crown octavo and which demy.

All books in Sections B, C and J–W are first editions in original state unless otherwise described.

---

[1] We have been at no pains to look for 'association copies' and very few are shown.

ACKNOWLEDGEMENTS

Without the guiding hand of Mr Sadleir in the choice of titles for each section, this exhibition would never have got beyond the blue-print stage. As for his provision of the major share of the books themselves, fellow-collectors will understand the risk of damage to such delicate material involved in packing and unpacking for a long journey, and installation even under the tenderest care; and they will join me in valuing his generosity accordingly.

I am much indebted also to Mr Dudley Massey, of Messrs Pickering & Chatto, for his advice on the selection and for reading the proofs of the catalogue; to Miss Edmondston, Librarian of the National Book League, for preparing the index; and to Mr Osbert Lancaster for designing the Railway Bookstall.

The portraits of Queen Victoria and the Prince Consort, from the royal collections at Marlborough House, have been graciously lent by HER MAJESTY QUEEN MARY.

JOHN CARTER

LOANS TO THE EXHIBITION

For the loan of such proportion of material as was required by the design of this exhibition, but was not available from Mr Sadleir's library, the organizers wish to record their indebtedness to the owners listed below. Thanks are specially due to the Librarian, Windsor Castle, and to the Antiquarian Booksellers' Association, whose Committee accorded full support and facilities.

HIS MAJESTY THE KING

Mrs Richard Bentley

Mr John Carter

Mr Richard Jennings

Mr Richard Sadleir

Miss Martha Smith

Mr Simon Nowell Smith

Major Hartley Clark

Mr H. W. Davies

Mr Arthur Dobell

Mr P. J. Dobell

Messrs J. A. D. Bridger

Messrs J. & E. Bumpus

Messrs William Dunlop

Messrs Francis Edwards

Messrs Elkin Mathews

Mr G. G. Elliott

Messrs Halewood & Son

Messrs Maggs Bros.

Messrs Marks & Co.

Messrs John Murray

Messrs Myers

Messrs Pickering & Chatto

Messrs Bernard Quaritch

Mr Arthur Rogers

Messrs Charles J. Sawyer

Messrs Scribners (New York)

Messrs W. T. Spencer

Messrs Stevens & Brown

Except where otherwise stated in the catalogue, however, *all books in the exhibition* and all the pictorial exhibits on the walls have been lent by

MR MICHAEL SADLEIR

A. *Magazine Serials*

A substantial proportion of Victorian fiction was first published serially in one of the numerous magazines. In the early days *Bentley's Miscellany*, *The Metropolitan*, *Ainsworth's* and the *Dublin University Magazine* were the most important media; but with the rise of Smith, Elder's *Cornhill* and its several rivals in the sixties the volume greatly increased. Whereas *Ainsworth's* and *The Metropolitan* (edited and largely occupied by Marryat) were authors' magazines, the later arrivals—*Tinsley's*, *Longman's*, *Macmillan's*, *St Paul's* (Virtue)—were predominantly publishers' ventures, which not only provided their promoters with a useful flow of new authors but also, by the combination of serial rights and book rights, enabled them to make attractive offers for the new work of established favourites.

The popularity of the part-issue (see Section B) reduced the contribution of some of the more successful writers, since the part-issue was a sort of serial itself; but even among these, a businesslike novelist like Trollope would spread his output over both fields, so that while *He Knew He was Right* was issued in parts in 1868/9 by Strahan, *Phineas Finn* was running at the same time in *St Paul's Magazine* before book publication in two volumes by Virtue.

Many of the magazine serials carried illustrations, which more often than not were omitted from the subsequent book edition (illustrated three-deckers are most exceptional), though one or two might reappear in a later reprint. And in some cases there were interesting differences of text between serialization and the book, of which *Tess of the D'Urbervilles* is one well-known example (serialized in *The Graphic*—with sections also appearing in *The Fortnightly* and in *The National Observer* —and published in 3 vols. by Osgood, McIlvaine in 1891—see Section J in this exhibition), and *Trilby* another (see Section V).

The initial retaliation of the magazines to part-issue competition took the form of reduction in price, from 2*s.* 6*d.* to 1*s.*; and if the part-issue in its hey-day (1840–1855) had attracted a heavy proportion of popular fiction, this opposition reacted in turn on its drawing power with the public, as Trollope makes clear in his *Autobiography*.[1] But it was the enterprise and profusion of the newer magazines which, in the years round 1860, began to cut seriously—and in the end decisively—into the part-issue's market, and the serial remained a dominant factor to the end of the century and beyond.

[1] Quoted by Graham Pollard in his essay, *Serial Fiction*, in *New Paths in Book Collecting* (Constable, 1934), the best introduction to the subject.

Of the many fiction-carrying magazines, some of which ran 'Annuals' as well, examples of the following are shown here:

B. *Part-issues*

The cheap reissue in 'numbers' of a popular work, whether of fiction or of moral instruction, had been a regular method of distribution since the early eighteenth century. Towards its end, publishers of a quite different type learned to spread the expense of big illustrated works—from Lavater's *Physiognomy* to Holbein's *Portraits*—over a period, by issue in parts. The former type, handled largely through hawkers and news-vendors at a few pence per issue, and the latter, subscribed for at prices up to a guinea a part by 'the nobility and gentry', were at the opposite economic poles of the publishing business; and though the middle area began to be tapped during the Regency by such works as *Dr Syntax's Tours*, these were still primarily picture books, with subsidiary text. It was in this tradition that 'in 1836 Chapman & Hall commissioned Robert Seymour to do some plates for a part-issue which was to be filled out with letterpress by an obscure journalist called Charles Dickens. The success of that letterpress—*The Posthumous Papers of the Pickwick Club*—changed the whole status of the part-issue for the next fifty years'.[1]

The vogue of the part-issue for best-selling fiction overtopped, but did not interfere with, its two earlier uses. It was due to other causes that the big topographical book declined in popularity after the classic period of the great aquatints, but such famous illustrated books as Dalziel's *Arabian Nights* and Doré's various editions continued to be published in parts.

[1] Graham Pollard, *op. cit.*, p. 261. The part-issue as a publishing form still awaits its historian; but Mr Pollard's essay on *Serial Fiction* gives a brief general analysis, while Mr Sadleir's *Trollope Bibliography* examines in detail the part-issue operations of an author whose publishers exploited every variety of the form for his prolific output.

The novel in parts was usually illustrated; one, two and sometimes even four plates by some popular artist being included in each number (the final part was usually a double number: i.e. 20 (say) in 19). It competed, as has already been noted, with the magazine serial, and temporary advantage was achieved now by one, now by the other. But from the late thirties to the early seventies the part-issue claimed a substantial share of the output of a dozen eminent and popular authors, including, for instance, every major novel of Dickens except *Oliver Twist* and *Great Expectations*, and of Thackeray except *Esmond* and *Philip*.

During the sixties, however, the magazine serial (with book publication in two or three volumes to follow) increased its drawing power decisively, and by the following decade the vogue for illustrating new fiction had also declined, so that although a few novels continued to be issued in parts even in the eighties, few important works of fiction were so published after 1870.

B **Dickens, Charles.** THE POSTHUMOUS PAPERS OF THE PICK-
1. WICK CLUB. Illustrated by R. Seymour and Phiz.

Chapman & Hall. 1836/7.

> (*a*) In the 20/19 monthly shilling parts (April 1836–November 1837).
> (*b*) 1 vol., cloth, plain style. Published at a guinea.
> *Pickwick* started slowly, sales of the first number (probably 1000) being so discouraging that only 500 of the second were printed. With the appearance of Sam Weller, popularity began and increased by leaps and bounds, so that first printings of the later parts ran well into five figures.
> *Pickwick* not only opened the eyes of publishers and authors to the possibilities of part-issue as a distributive method, but also set the physical style for many of its successors.
> *Lent by Messrs J. & E. Bumpus and Messrs Pickering & Chatto.*

2. **Marryat, Captain Frederick.** POOR JACK. With illustrations by Clarkson Stanfield.

Longmans. 1840.

> (*a*) Twelve shilling parts, published monthly, January–December 1840.
> (*b*) 1 vol., cloth. Published 1 December 1840 at 14*s*.
> The cloth volume is a characteristic example of the decorated style, with appropriate pictorial or emblematical designs in gilt, which is found on many part-issued novels of this period.

3. **Thackeray, W. M.** THE HISTORY OF PENDENNIS. Illustrated by the author.

Bradbury & Evans. 1848/50.

> (*a*) In the 24/23 monthly parts.
> (*b*) In 2 vols., cloth.
> The style of the parts, with a woodcut vignette, is typical of the part-issues of Dickens, Thackeray and Surtees, each of whom, however, had his regular coloured paper as a sort of trade-mark—Dickens, greeny blue; Thackeray, yellow; Surtees, brick red.

3 (*continued*)

The cloth volumes are of plain style equally characteristic, in colour and 'blind' decoration, of Thackeray's part-issued novels, just as *Nicholas Nickleby* (see P 1) is of Dickens's; whereas Surtees's publishers followed the pictorially decorated tradition of Ainsworth and Marryat. *Parts lent by Messrs Halewood & Son. Volumes by Messrs W. T. Spencer.*

4.   Trollope, Anthony. HE KNEW HE WAS RIGHT. With 64 illustrations by Marcus Stone.

Virtue. 1868/9.

(*a*) Thirty-two sixpenny parts, published weekly, 17 October 1868–22 May 1869. In April Virtue, in financial straits, sold the copyright to Strahan, but his imprint persists to the end of the part-issue.

(*b*) 2 vols., cloth. Published May 1869 at £1. 1*s*. with Strahan's imprint.

The weekly parts show a combination of the use of colour and an illustration (not, incidentally, reproduced in the book edition). The decorative style of the two volumes is formal, for the use of pictorial blocking (cf. B2 above) had by now gone out of fashion for the volume form of part-issued novels.

5.   'Eliot, George' (= Marian Evans, afterwards Cross). MIDDLEMARCH. A STUDY OF PROVINCIAL LIFE.

Edinburgh and London: Blackwood. 1871/2.

(*a*) Eight five-shilling parts, published at irregular intervals between December 1871 and December 1872.

(*b*) 4 vols., cloth. Published at £2. 2*s*. The title-page of the first volume is dated 1871, the remainder 1872.

This smaller-sized and more expensive type of part-issue never achieved much popularity, though it was used by Blackwood for the same author's *Daniel Deronda* (1876) and by Chapman & Hall for Trollope's *The Prime Minister* (1876). 'Presumably the suppression of the sixpenny or shilling crown 8vo part was a concession to public weariness of frequent short instalments of a popular fiction' (Sadleir, *Trollope, a Bibliography*, p. 154), and an attitude of concession to library requirements was shown by the concurrent issue in cloth of the parts both of *Middlemarch* and *Daniel Deronda*. But the vogue of the part-issue was over, and these compromises did not avail to revive it.

6.   Viles, E. (attributed to). BLACK BESS, OR THE KNIGHT OF THE ROAD.

E. Harrison. (*c.* 1880.)

254 penny parts, published weekly.

Described as the third reissue in this form of a popular favourite, this is a typical example of those cheap part-issues, aimed largely at the schoolboy market, which continued, along-side (and by this time, outliving) their newly respectable brethren, the original tradition of the part-issue as distributed through the chapbook and newsvending trades. The garish folding colour plates which accompany the early issues soon give way to monochrome and shortly disappear altogether, their place being taken periodically by a free sample of Part 1 of some other publication.   *Lent by Messrs Scribners.*

C. *Three-deckers*

Three small octavo volumes had become, during the first quarter of the nineteenth century, the standard form for fiction publishing; and though the page size had increased slightly between *Pride and Prejudice* (1813) and *The Last Days of Pompeii* (1834) the format had changed little in other respects. During the Victorian age, though a certain number of unillustrated[1] novels were published in two volumes and a very few in one or four, the three-decker convention was maintained, largely through the influence of the circulating libraries, whose patrons liked to feel they were getting their money's worth of reading. The public's appetite for ample reading, the three-decker convention and the requirements of the serial and the part-issue all influenced writers towards a leisurely length. It was only in the eighties that medium-length novels began to be artificially spun out to three volumes, and the physical conventions did not long survive the swing away, both in readers and writers, from the spacious, many-plotted novel of mid-Victorian days towards a shorter and more astringent formula.

That for two decades after 1837 the outward appearance of the three-decker changed very little, in spite of the establishment during the thirties of gilt-lettered and gilt-decorated cloth bindings in other departments of publishing, was due to the peculiar methods of fiction distribution. For besides the bulk purchases of the libraries, novels were commonly handled in large wholesale lots by jobbers: and both were as likely to buy from the publisher in quires as in boards or half-cloth, for binding on their own account. Consequently, the publisher had little reason to spend money or attention on beautifying his fiction output, and with few exceptions the exterior of the three-decker remained sober —indeed often drab—by comparison with other books until the end of the fifties.

Even then, when fiction had fallen into line with general books in discarding half-cloth for full-cloth, gilt, the three-decker as a whole tended for some years to lag behind in respect of care and taste in the treatment of its exterior; and though Bentley, Smith Elder and Chapman & Hall maintained a respectable style, the tradition that it did not matter much what novels looked like died particularly hard in firms like Newby, Hurst & Blackett or Tinsley which published very little else. Exceptions to this rule, however, became increasingly widespread, and during the last quarter of the century the three-decker, in its economic decadence, blossomed out into a riot of competitive gaiety, with the great fiction house of Bentley leading the field in ingenuity and extravagance.

---

[1] For the illustrated novel, issued in parts, see the previous Section.

By the nineties novels published in one volume at 6*s*. (4*s*. 6*d*. net cash) decisively outnumbered the three-deckers, and the margin for lavish detail in production had disappeared. No 'functional' section in the present exhibition has been devoted to these, but a number of examples may be seen in Sections J–W.

C   **Brougham, Henry.** ALBERT LUNEL.

1.   3 vols. Charles Knight. 1844.

> All-over drab boards, paper labels.
> This, the standard dress of novels during the Regency period, persisted long past the introduction of publisher's cloth (*c*. 1825), and though it became steadily less common during the forties, examples even survive from the following decade.

2.   **Norton, Caroline.** STUART OF DUNLEATH. A STORY OF MODERN TIMES.

3 vols. Colburn. 1851.

> (*a*) Boards, cloth backs, paper labels.
> (*b*) Full cloth, lettered in gilt.
> These alternative styles for fiction (published at the same price) ran concurrently for a number of years. Novels were marketed largely through wholesalers, who often (until the fifties at any rate) bought in quires and did their own binding; and so did the lending libraries until full cloth became stabilized as the only binding for fiction (late fifties).
> The concurrent style proper lasted from the mid-thirties to the mid-forties; but it was revived only a few years later owing to shortages of cloth and persisted, for economic reasons rather than from choice, till the late fifties. Trollope's *The Three Clerks*, for instance, was issued both in full cloth and half-cloth in 1858.

3.   **Brotherton, Mary.** ARTHUR BRANDON.

2 vols. Hurst & Blackett. 1856.

> This two-volume novel has been deliberately intruded here as a reminder that exceptions to the three-volume standard, though a small minority, were not infrequent. The grey-green cloth and its rather commonplace treatment are typical of the routine novel in the middle years of the century.

4.   **Moodie, Mrs.** THE WORLD BEFORE THEM.

3 vols. Bentley. 1868.

> Maroon or claret-coloured cloth was a favourite for fiction at this period, and its treatment here, though still unambitious, shows some signs of self-respect.

5.   **Fitzgerald, Percy.** THE PARVENU FAMILY, OR PHOEBE, GIRL AND WIFE.

3 vols. Bentley. 1876.

> This diagonally ribbed cloth was popular in the seventies, and the combination of colour and decoration has begun to give a brisker general effect.

6.   **Moore, George.** A MODERN LOVER.

3 vols. Tinsley. 1883.

The all-powerful Mudie banned this book from his shelves, which was enough to kill any three-decker. The author, however, found a champion in Vizetelly, a publisher less dependent than a routine fiction house like Tinsley on lending-library good will, and his next book (see M 11) was issued in one volume at 6s., so that those who could not borrow could buy (and for 4s. 6d. if they liked to pay cash, a discount which remained normal till the Net Book Agreement in 1899). He also attacked Mudie in a pamphlet, a copy of which is shown, entitled *Literature at Nurse, or Circulating Morals.*

In the atmosphere of publicity provoked by the case, the artificially high price of the three-decker was thus brought forcibly to public attention, and although it lingered on for a decade, it was doomed. By the nineties the ordinary novel was normally published in one volume instead of three and at 6s. instead of £1. 11s. 6d.

7.   **'Maartens, Maarten'** (=Joost M. W. van der Poorten Schwartz). THE GREATER GLORY.

3 vols. Bentley. 1894.

If the three-decker was to die, the great fiction firm of Bentley was determined that it should die gloriously. The bronze-butterflied design here covers the edges as well as the binding itself and demonstrates the large margin for frills which lay between the printing cost and the wholesale selling price of the three-decker. The discount to the lending libraries was 50%, and a publisher and his author could make a respectable profit with a sale as low as 1000 copies. Since Mudie took 1500 of any Bentley novel, sight unseen, there was plenty of margin for butterflies, silk bows, chintz and inset calling cards.

8.   **Wingfield, The Hon. Lewis.** THE MAID OF HONOUR.

3 vols. Bentley. 1891.

Another typical Bentley three-decker of the final period.

9.   **Library Copies.**

As a reminder of the condition to which the vast majority of three-deckers were reduced by library circulation, and in which they normally survive to-day, three specimens are here shown.

Of two copies of Hardy's first novel *Desperate Remedies* (3 vols. Tinsley, 1871), one is in that dingy half roan, marbled paper sides, which is familiar on library-bound fiction from the twenties to the eighties; the other has been cut down and put into plain 'binder's cloth', with 'Mudie's Select Library' on the spine of the first volume.

The third example is *Ayala's Angel* by Anthony Trollope (3 vols. Chapman & Hall, 1881), the front covers of which are defaced by the pink printed labels of Lawrence's Library, Rugby.

10. 'Remainders'

An unsuccessful three-decker might be sold off, in quires or bound, to a remainder publisher, or to a circulating library for its less fastidious country branches (cf. note to E2). The latter would normally keep it in three volumes, for obvious reasons; but the former often economized by binding up three volumes in one, sometimes with the original price of 31*s*. 6*d*. prominently stamped on the spine, for contrast with the reduced price on the flyleaf. The example of this degraded thing shown here is *Restless Human Hearts* by Richard Jefferies. originally published in 3 vols. by Tinsley in 1875.

D. *One-volume Reprints*

The Victorian novelist normally sold his product to a publisher for an outright sum, for the royalty system urged on authors by Sir Walter Besant's 'Authors' Society' and by A. P. Watt, the first of the powerful 'literary agents', was virtually unknown before the 'eighties and was not firmly established till the final years of our period. But just as he might sell the serial rights separately if his publisher did not also (as many did) operate a magazine, so he would often sell the book rights either for a term of years (Meredith, for instance, sold *Diana of the Crossways* for five years for £500 to Chapman & Hall), or for three-volume publication only: the reprint and cheap-edition rights being subject to later negotiations and further payment. These alternative practices affected, in various ways, both the interval between the original publication and the first cheap reprint and also the form and price of that reprint, even though the novel's initial success and its consequent expectation of purchasers (as distinct from borrowers) remained the dominating factor. In general, however, it was one result of an artificial convention that the interval between the original three- or two-decker and its first cheap edition, whether in one of the reprint series or independently, was normally much shorter than has become customary in the present century—often less than a year, sometimes no more than six months. Similarly revealing of the deliberate exploitation of the library market was the reduction in price—31*s*. 6*d*. or £1. 1*s*. to 6*s*. or 5*s*.—proportionately much greater than that between 7*s*. 6*d*. and 3*s*. 6*d*., the standard comparative figures of the years between the two world wars.

The Victorian fiction reprint series are shown in the following section. The present comprises a small selection of individual reprints characteristic of their periods in general and of their publishers in particular.

1.   **Gaskell, Mrs.** MY LADY LUDLOW, AND OTHER TALES. Sampson, Low. 1861.

First published in 1859 in 2 vols., under the title *Round the Sofa*.

2. **Trollope, Anthony.** THE KELLYS AND THE O'KELLYS.
Chapman & Hall. 1862.

> First published in 3 vols. by Colburn in 1848. This reprint was uniform
> with a number of other Trollope titles reissued during his 'Chapman &
> Hall' period (1858 to 1866). *Lent by John Carter.*

3. **Norton, Caroline.** LOST AND SAVED.
Hurst & Blackett. 1863.

4. **Wood, Mrs Henry.** VERNER'S PRIDE.
Bradbury & Evans. 1864.

> First published in 3 vols. in 1863.

5. **Edwards, Amelia B.** HALF A MILLION OF MONEY.
Tinsley. 1866.

> First published in 3 vols. earlier in the same year.

6. **Braddon, Miss M. E.** BIRDS OF PREY.
Ward, Lock & Tyler. 1868.

> First published in 3 vols. in 1867.

7. **Marryat, Florence.** LOVE'S CONFLICT.
Warne. 1869.

> First published by Bentley, 3 vols., 1865. *Lent by Mrs Richard Bentley.*

8. **Mulock, Dinah Maria (Mrs Craik).** THE HEAD OF THE
FAMILY.
Macmillan. 1875.

> First published by Chapman & Hall, 3 vols., 1852.

9. **Collins, Wilkie.** AFTER DARK.
Smith, Elder. 1888.

> First published in 1865, in 2 vols.

10. **Hardy, Thomas.** UNDER THE GREENWOOD TREE.
Chatto & Windus. 1891.

> Originally published in 2 vols. in 1872, this had been reprinted in 1 vol.
> by Tinsley in 1876. The present reprint was included in Chatto &
> Windus's 'Piccadilly Library'.

11. **James, Henry.** THE TRAGIC MUSE.
Macmillan. 1891.

> First published in 1890, in 3 vols.

12. **Cholmondeley, Mary.** THE DANVERS JEWELS.
Bentley. 1898.

> First published in 1887. The gold flower decoration on white cloth of
> this reprint shows the influence of the *Art Nouveau* style.
> *Lent by Mrs Richard Bentley.*

E. Fiction Series

The immediate impulse in England to fiction reprints in handy form, at a reasonable price and on a large scale, came, like so many other English impulses, from Scotland. For although cheap reissues of the classics had not been infrequent, from Harrison's *Novelist's Magazine* (1789–1791) to Whittingham's *Pocket Novelists* (1825–1828), it was Cadell's *Author's Edition of the Waverley Novels*, which began to appear at 5*s.* a volume in 1829, that first applied the same method to the recent works of a living, if however exceptional, writer. In the matter of format Cadell had no doubt been influenced by the neat glazed canvas and paper labels of *Constable's Miscellany* (1827 onwards), and it was in such general literature, not fiction, that Cadell's own example was most immediately followed. Murray's *Family Library*, the *Cabinet Cyclopedia* of Dr Lardner (Longmans) and the *Library of Entertaining Knowledge* of Charles Knight, were only three of a number of small cloth-bound non-fiction series, selling for 5*s.* a volume, which were well under way by 1830.

In 1831 the formula was applied to fiction, with the first volumes of Colburn & Bentley's (soon Bentley's alone) *Standard Novels*, the original announcement of which duly acknowledged its parentage—the *Waverley Novels* of Cadell. The series was immediately successful; and its careful selection, respectful editing and enterprising distribution not only established it in a long and fruitful career, but inspired several imitators, one of whom (as will be seen below) capitalized unscrupulously on Bentley's standards without attempting to emulate them.

From 1832 to 1846 Bentley, Colburn (now independent) and Blackwood had the fiction series field to themselves. In the latter year Simms & McIntyre of Belfast introduced their *Parlour Novelist* series, at 2*s.* 6*d.* a volume as against the ruling 6*s.*; and in 1847 they followed up this trial balloon by *The Parlour Library*, which, at 1*s.* in boards and 1*s.* 6*d.* in cloth, was an innovation as revolutionary as Bentley's of fifteen years before. This further reduction in the cheap series price, together with other features noted below, brought Bentley's and Colburn's price down, and opened the eyes of a number of other publishers—Routledge in particular—to the possibilities of the new market. As with Bentley in 1831, so Simms & McIntyre, the innovatiors of 1847, never lost their head start, and *The Parlour Library*, with its 320 pages for 1*s.* and a number of original works among its reprints, had a long and successful, as well as a highly influential career. But there was plenty of room for others, even if they lacked the same imagination and enterprise, and Routledge's *Railway Library* probably ran up a longer list of titles than any other cheap reprint series in the history of publishing.

Later series were numerous, and tended to concentrate on two distinct markets: the 1*s*. or 2*s*., yellow-back style, reprint for railway or other ephemeral reading, and the 5*s*. or 6*s*. edition for bookshop sale to those who liked to own and re-read what they had first borrowed from the library. These latter, often well printed and solidly bound (*Bentley's Favourite Novels* is a good, if rather favourable, representative), were the forerunners of the *Traveller's* or *New Adelphi Libraries* of our own day, whereas the *Parlour* and *Railway Libraries* were the ancestors of *Nelson's Sevenpennies* or *Penguin*. Distinguished exceptions to the general run were Macmillan's *Illustrated Standard Novels* (1895–1901), which is shown in Section F, and John Lane's *Keynotes Series*, examples of which conclude the present section.

E Bentley's Standard Novels, 1831–1855.

1. Certainly the most influential and probably still the most famous series of cheap novels in the history of English publishing, Bentley's *Standard Novels* began in 1831 with Fenimore Cooper's *The Pilot*. '*The Pilot* for six shillings!' exclaimed *The Spectator*. 'This is indeed a phenomenon in the history of literature.' Before its demise in 1855, the series had run to 126 vols., changing its dress three times to conform to stylistic developments.

   The volumes shown here represent:
   A. Nos. 1–70 (1831–1838).
   B. Nos. 71–80 (1838–1840).
   C. Nos. 81–114 (1840–1848).
   D. Nos. 115–126 (1849–1855).

   The first 19 vols. bore the imprint of Colburn & Bentley: but when the partnership was dissolved in 1832, Bentley retained the series. The original conception called for the inclusion of correct texts of the great eighteenth-century novels: many volumes by living writers gave a revised text and an introduction: and it was only towards the end that the *Standard Novels* became frankly a cheap-edition series of Bentley's contemporary best-sellers—the first sustained attempt, incidentally, at this form of exploitation.

   Each volume contained an engraved frontispiece, and vols. 1–92 an engraved title-page as well. The original price of 6*s*. was later reduced to 5*s*., and subsequent reissues were priced at 3*s*. 6*d*. In the later forties there was a temporary period of further drastic price cutting to meet the competition of *The Parlour Library* (see below).

   Bentley's outlay on the series by 1849, when 116 vols. had been issued, was stated by *The Morning Herald* to have been £88,000, and the publisher's own figure for the entire series was 'close upon £100,000'.

2. Colburn's Modern Novelists, 1831–1836 and Standard Novels, 1835–1848.

Henry Colburn was a sort of Rupert of Hentzau of the publishing business: a promoter and operator of great ingenuity and not much principle. After some years of business on his own he had in 1829

2 *(continued)*

entered into an uneasy partnership with Bentley (a very different type of man) on a three-year agreement, which was not renewed in 1832.

The original announcement of Bentley's *Standard Novels* had been made over the joint imprint; and though the imaginative and scholarly conception of the series was almost certainly Bentley's, Colburn was quick to capitalize on its success by launching, independently, several series which were as different in real as they were similar in superficial intentions. For where Bentley's *Standard Novels* were a creative series of successful books, carefully edited, Colburn's first venture, the *Modern Novelists* series, was no more than a method of disposing of unsold stock, often of unsuccessful titles—a sort of remaindering operation disguised as a proprietary series. The pretence of monthly issue did not last long, and by December 1836 the 190 vols. to which the series had been raised by the increased flood of 'remainders' were being frankly advertised as 'cheap editions adapted for country libraries'.

In 1836 Colburn tried a new reprint series of popular titles from his own list. With *Colburn's Standard Novelists* (which in the end became *Novels*) he imitated Bentley's format, printed genuinely fresh editions, discontinued his earlier attempts to undercut his late partner with a 5s. price, resorted when convenient to unannounced abridgement of the longer books, and devoted enough of his undoubted promotional talent to the series to carry it successfully on till 1848. Two years later he sold it, name and all, to Tegg, a publisher who specialized in remainders.

Examples are shown here of the seven successive formats in which the two series were put out, together with an example of the weekly parts in which alternative form the first half-dozen titles in the *Standard Novelists* were also issued.

3. Routledge's Standard Novels, 1851–*c*.1860.

Although tastefully launched as a series 'published from time to time and comprising Bijoux of Romance and Standard Works of Celebrated Authors', this was really not so much a series, in the creative sense of Bentley or Simms & McIntyre, as a miscellaneous collection of cheap editions of popular fiction to which a series title was, for marketing reasons, rather fitfully applied. The early titles were reissues of works which had previously appeared in 2 vols. or 2 series in the *Railway Library*; a number of later ones were taken over from Bentley (and printed from Bentley plates, if not actually Bentley sheets); and before the end renumbering and other irregularities confuse the sequence.

Routledge's Standard Novels, like their *Railway Library* (see no. 5 below) an imitative series, were published at 2s. 6d. a volume. The format was twice changed, and all three varieties are shown here.

4. Simms & McIntyre's Parlour Library, 1847–1863.

The sensational importance—in its courage, efficiency of handling and success—of the *Parlour Library* as an innovation in cheap book publishing has hardly been realized. Its most remarkable feature was, perhaps, its sponsorship: for it originated in Ireland, with a firm of printers who had no experience of general publishing, and had no London money or support behind it. Its success was immediate and overwhelming. A London office was soon opened, and in 1853 the original promoters sold out to their London agent, Thomas Hodgson. By the time the *Parlour Library*, after further transfers of ownership, disappeared about 1863, nearly 300 titles had been issued.

The series was revolutionary in two ways. It began with a *new* work of fiction by one of the best Irish writers, William Carleton; and although the majority of later titles were reprints, it continued to include a substantial proportion of original work, first translations, etc. This was a radical difference from the only proprietary fiction series existing in 1846—Bentley's, Colburn's and Blackwood's. The second sensational feature was the price: 1*s.* in boards, 1*s.* 6*d.* in cloth, against the 5*s.* or 6*s.* of the others; and it is the measure of the impression made by these two Belfast printers on the London market that within three or four years Bentley & Colburn reduced their series price to 3*s.* 6*d.* and then to 2*s.* 6*d.*, Chapman & Hall had started their *Select Library* at 2*s.*, and Routledge's *Railway Library* was already a dozen volumes old, at *Parlour* price and in a close imitation of its format.

The *Parlour Library* put the shilling novel on the map, and its decorated board covers (from which the cover of the present catalogue is adapted) paved the technical way to the shortly omnipresent 'yellow-back'

Incidentally, the career of the series strikingly exemplifies the influence an intelligent publisher, who takes his job seriously, can exert on such a venture: and, conversely, how rapidly a mere profit-hound can ruin a good thing. So long as Simms & McIntyre were in charge (and their influence lasted well into the Hodgson regime as the result of forward contracts) the series was orderly, skilfully mixed and enterprising. But the later Hodgson period, and still more the various regimes which followed, reduced the *Parlour Library* in the end to a chaos of second-rate reprints.

5.   Routledge's Railway Library, 1849 onwards.

This long-lived, prolific and enormously successful series has often been regarded as a pioneer venture in cheap book publishing. Actually it was a conscious imitation of the *Parlour Library*, both in appearance and sales-appeal; but its huge output—the list for 1862 runs to 327 titles, that for 1880 to 860—bestrode the bookstall market for decades and its name became a household word.

The preliminary announcement was a fine example of 'publisherese'. 'It is not only the best intellects of other nations, and the fresh genius of the New World [the first title was Cooper's *The Pilot*], that is now being brought into play, but, be it remembered, some of the imperishable charms of our own dear native literature.'

The full original title was *The Railway Library and Fireside Companion*, and the monthly volumes were issued at 1*s.* in 'fancy boards' and 1*s.* 6*d.* in cloth. The style of the former was modified as the years went by to conform to contemporary publishing fashions: representative examples of both styles and several periods are shown here.

6.   Tales From Blackwood. First Series 1858–1861, Second Series 1879–1881, Third Series 1889–1890.

Edinburgh was ten years behind London with the fiction reprint series, and Blackwood's *Standard Novels*, though planned and produced with

6 (*continued*)

exemplary care, only ran to fourteen titles before being discontinued in 1843. But in 1858 Blackwood turned the tables on Bentley with a project for collecting, in a series of low-priced volumes, the best stories from his famous magazine. Bentley replied in 1859, with *Tales from Bentley*, but retired after two years: while *Tales from Blackwood* continued, at intervals, for 32, and eventually totalled 30 vols.

The *First Series* (1858–1861) was issued in sixpenny monthly parts and in 12 quarterly cloth volumes at 1*s*. 6*d*. each; the *Second Series* (1879–1881) in shilling monthly parts and 12 vols., together at the conclusion of the part-issue, at 2*s*. 6*d*. each; the *Third Series* (1889–1890) in 12 monthly shilling parts and 6 vols. at 2*s*. 6*d*. each. A selection of the parts and cloth volumes are shown here.

Tales from Blackwood contained verse and occasionally an essay or dramatic piece: but it was mainly devoted to short stories.

7.   Bentley's Favourite Novels, 1863–1897.

This series, published at 6*s*., carried the tradition of the *Standard Novels* to the end of the firm's life. It did not compete with the really cheap series, but bridged the gap between these and the three-decker for those who wanted a presentable and decently printed edition to keep on their shelves. As with the earlier series, a considerable number of revised texts testify to the editorial care of the publisher, and towards the end, when new novels at 6*s*. were becoming frequent, a certain number of original works were included among the reprints (see, for instance, N 26 in the present exhibition).

A special catalogue of the series issued in 1886 runs to 32 pages and lists 109 titles, to which half a dozen or more were normally added during each succeeding publishing season.

8.   John Lane's Keynotes Series, 1893–1897.

This was by far the most elegant fiction series of the nineteenth century, and it differs from all the others shown in this section in that it was devoted not to reprints but to original works. As was natural from the most ninetyish of the publishers of the nineties, its slim format, excellent paper and printing, the careful choice of colours for cloth and decoration and the binding designs by Beardsley and others combined to produce volumes which were stylish without being too affected, *soignés* yet solid and readable.

33 vols. were issued, at 3*s*. 6*d*. each. It was originally intended to issue the series in wrappers, not cloth, and the first volume, *Keynotes* by George Egerton, was so published. A copy of this is shown here, alongside a selection of volumes in cloth.

F. *Illustrators*

Illustration was a frequent and influential ingredient in Victorian book-making in general. As for fiction, though three-deckers were very rarely illustrated, it had its fair share in magazine serials, in part-issued form, and also in later reprints. The early years of our period were dominated by Cruikshank, Hablot K. Browne (Phiz), Leech and their followers: later, though the great illustrators of the sixties concentrated on poetry and bestowed much of their best work on the magazines, Millais, du Maurier, Marcus Stone and others illustrated novels: while the later years of the century produced a heavy crop of illustrated fiction reprints, led by Macmillan with the *Cranford* and *Illustrated Standard Novels Series*, which showed to advantage the work of Hugh Thomson, Fred Pegram and other artists in line.

The selection of books shown here is a small one, since much of the best fiction illustration was done for the magazines. Some examples of these are shown, together with a number of proofs from the Smith, Elder collection, now in Mr Sadleir's library. Also on the walls are a number of specimens of colour illustrations, including prospectuses, designs for pictorial board bindings, etc., from the files of that prince of colour printers, Edmund Evans; also from Mr Sadleir's collection.

1. **Dickens, Charles.** THE ADVENTURES OF OLIVER TWIST. Illustrated by **George Cruikshank.**

    3 vols. Bentley. 1838.

    Some of Cruikshank's most famous illustrations appear in this example of that rare phenomenon, an illustrated three-decker.
    Lent by Messrs Pickering & Chatto.

2. **Marryat, Capt. Frederick.** JACOB FAITHFUL. Illustrated by **Robert Buss.**

    3 vols. Saunders & Otley. 1839.

    The publishers' project for a complete illustrated edition of Marryat, of which this and *Peter Simple* only were produced, was unfortunately abandoned. The bindings as well as the coloured plates are particularly successful.
    The 1928 reprint, with plates and binding in facsimile, is also shown.

3. **Carleton, William.** TRAITS AND STORIES OF THE IRISH PEASANTRY. New edition illustrated by **Phiz (Hablot K. Browne), Sibson, Wrightson, Franklin, Macmanus, Lee** and **Gilbert.**

    2 vols. Dublin: Curry. 1843.

15

4.   Surtees, Robert Smith. HANDLEY CROSS, OR THE SPA HUNT. Illustrated by **John Leech.**

Bradbury & Evans. 1854.

Originally published in 3 vols. in 1843, unillustrated, *Handley Cross* had very little success. The popularity of *Mr Jorrocks's Sporting Tours* in magazine form with coloured plates by Alken suggested the use of Leech for the reissue of *Handley Cross* and the first publication of most of Surtees's other novels; and the combination was a popular success from the start.   *Lent by HIS MAJESTY THE KING.*

5.   Trollope, Anthony. ORLEY FARM. Illustrated by **J. E. Millais.**

2 vols. Chapman & Hall. 1862.   *Lent by Richard Jennings.*

6.   Jerrold, Douglas. MRS CAUDLE'S CURTAIN LECTURES. Illustrated by **Charles Keene.**

Bradbury & Evans. 1866   *Lent by Messrs Francis Edwards.*

7.   Trollope, Anthony. HE KNEW HE WAS RIGHT. Illustrated by **Marcus Stone.**

2 vols. Strahan. 1869.   *Lent by Richard Jennings.*

8.   Montgomery, Florence. MISUNDERSTOOD. Illustrated by **George du Maurier.**

Bentley. 1874.

9.   Bulwer, Edward (Lord Lytton). THE PARISIANS. Covers designed by **Walter Crane.**

2 vols. Routledge. (*c.* 1885.)   *Lent by John Carter.*

10.   Gaskell, Mrs. CRANFORD. Illustrated by **Hugh Thomson.**

Macmillan. 1891.

This was the most popular of the publishers' series of reprints, illustrated in black and white and handsomely bound in green and gold, which became known as the *Cranford Series*. Several other publishers paid it the compliment of imitation (see T. Balston, *English Book Illustration 1880–1890* in *New Paths in Book-Collecting* for details). The *Cranford Series* sold for 6*s.* a volume.

11.   Marryat, Capt. Frederick. MASTERMAN READY. Illustrated by **Fred Pegram.**

Macmillan. 1897.

The *Illustrated Standard Novels*, an admirable series, were issued in two styles—plain red cloth, with untrimmed edges, and blue cloth lavishly decorated in gold with peacock end papers in yellow and white and gilt edges. Both varieties are shown here.

12.   Brontë, Charlotte. SHIRLEY. Illustrated by **F. H. Townsend.**

Service & Paton. 1897.   *Lent by Mr H. W. Davies.*

G. *The Railway Bookstall*

The railway bookstall was perhaps the most important outlet and display stand for the numerous cheap fiction series, yellow-backs[1] and the like. Several reprint series, indeed, were avowedly dedicated to train reading, as their titles show (see Section E). In order to give some idea of the liveliness and variety of these, a miniature pastiche of such a bookstall has been designed for this exhibition by the learned and ingenious Mr Osbert Lancaster; and on its shelves and counter are set out a number of books, periodicals, etc., such as would have been available to the traveller at some not too precise date between 1860 and 1880.

The *Railway Libraries, Run and Read Libraries* and their kind were often ill printed on poor paper and they must have been a severe strain on the reader's eyes, whether jogging in the train or at home. But they had this in common with their descendants to-day, that their exteriors did what they could to attract the buyer's attention; and if the designs were sometimes commonplace, they were often vigorous, while the common tendency to a colour scheme based on red, yellow and black gave a certain homogeneity to a good rowdy tradition.

H. *The Parlour Bookcase*

In Section C we have given a bird's-eye view of the development of the three-decker during the Victorian age, and a considerable number of other examples are on view elsewhere in the exhibition. None of these individual examples, however, can provide more than a hint of what novels looked like *in bulk*, as they might have been seen at any time during our period in a publisher's office, a really well-stocked bookshop or the parlour of, shall we say, a family with half a dozen fiction-reading daughters, rich enough and unconventional enough to buy novels instead of getting them from the library.

We have therefore arranged here, without regard to their contents, a collection of almost a hundred three-deckers, ranging in date from the fifties to the end of the century. Mostly published by Richard Bentley & Son, they nevertheless represent a fair enough cross-section of the fiction of the period, and they give some idea of the spaciousness, variety and solid workmanship of novel-publishing in late Victorian times.

The Bentley selection were once part of the publisher's file set, and have been lent to the exhibition by Messrs Maggs Bros.

[1] The best account of the origins and development of the 'yellow-back' is Mr Sadleir's essay in *New Paths in Book Collecting*.

I. Current Reprints

The public appetite for reprints of Victorian fiction has been growing, but the publishers' ability to satisfy it has been frustrated of recent years by the general shortage of paper and production facilities. Consequently the selection of current editions shown here is smaller and less varied than it would have been ten years ago, and much smaller, it may be hoped, than it would be five years hence. But the Victorians have had their share of available production; and if the palm must go to the Oxford University Press for the constancy of their *World's Classics Series'* devotion to Trollope, *Everyman* is a worthy competitor, and there are many other encouraging signs that the reprinting of Victorian novelists is on the increase.

J. The Giants

As has been pointed out in the Introduction, this selection of major writers makes no claim to be above criticism. It represents what the organizers of the exhibition regard as a reasonable aristocracy of Victorian novelists, once the right has been admitted to reserve for other, more specific categories some authors who might be thought, in their own right, to rank with the dozen who follow. The titles chosen to represent the 'Giants' are, so far as possible, *key-titles*, in the sense of being universally known. They are not offered as the greatest or even best, though several would be hardly disputed; nor are they necessarily the rarest, although more than half of them are certainly the most 'difficult' of the important works in their writer's bibliographies, and two or three will only be seen once in a lifetime in fine original condition.

1. **Dickens, Charles.** THE POSTHUMOUS PAPERS OF THE PICK-WICK CLUB. Illustrated by R. Seymour and Phiz.
    Chapman & Hall. 1866.

    This reprint of *Pickwick* bears a presentation inscription from the author to Queen Victoria. A set of the original part-issue, as published in 1836/7, is shown in Section B.   *Lent by HIS MAJESTY THE KING.*

2. **Thackeray, W. M.** VANITY FAIR. A NOVEL WITHOUT A HERO. Illustrated by the author.
    Bradbury & Evans. 1847/8.

    The original 20/19 shilling parts, issued monthly from January 1847 onwards. Also published in one volume, cloth, at a guinea.
    Lent by Messrs Stevens & Brown.

3.   **The Brontë Sisters.**

(*a*) WUTHERING HEIGHTS, by Ellis Bell, 2 vols.
AGNES GREY, by Acton Bell, 1 vol.

3 vols. T. C. Newby. 1847.

Published together in the format of an ordinary three-volume novel, concurrently in half cloth (as shown here) with paper labels and in full cloth (see note to C2). This is one of the rarest of all Victorian novels in fine original condition.

(*b*) JANE EYRE. AN AUTOBIOGRAPHY. Edited by Currer Bell.

3 vols. Smith, Elder. 1847.

The almost simultaneous publication of the masterpieces of the two sisters, with Anne's *Agnes Grey* as a makeweight to Emily's, took place in the year following the notably unsuccessful volume of poems to which all three had contributed.

4.   **Gaskell, Mrs.** CRANFORD.

Chapman & Hall. 1853.

The author's fourth novel.

5.   **Trollope, Anthony.** BARCHESTER TOWERS.

3 vols. Longmans. 1857.

This was the author's fifth novel, the second of the Barchester series (*The Warden* had been published in 1855), and his first real success.

6.   **'Eliot, George'.** ADAM BEDE.

3 vols. Edinburgh and London: Blackwood. 1859.

Adam Bede, following *Scenes of Clerical Life* at a year's interval, was the author's first major work of fiction.

7.   **Meredith, George.** THE ORDEAL OF RICHARD FEVEREL.

3 vols. Chapman & Hall. 1859.

The year 1859 was a remarkable one in literary history; it saw the first publication, besides the two novels shown here, of Dickens's *A Tale of Two Cities*, Henry Kingsley's *Geoffrey Hamlyn*, Darwin's *Origin of Species*, Tennyson's *Idylls of the King*, Fitzgerald's translation of *The Rubaiyat*, Smiles's *Self Help* and the early numbers of Mrs Beeton's *Book of Household Cookery*.

8.   **Collins, Wilkie.** THE WOMAN IN WHITE.

3 vols. Sampson Low. 1860.

The Woman in White, the author's fifth novel, was serialized in *All the Year Round* and in *Harper's Weekly*. An American edition was immediately printed from the text of the latter magazine and it is uncertain whether this or the first English edition appeared the earlier. Mr Brussel, in *Anglo-American First Editions*, gave priority to the Harper edition, but Mr Parrish, in *Victorian Lady Novelists*, reversed the order.

9. **Le Fanu, Joseph Sheridan.** UNCLE SILAS. A TALE OF BAR-
    TRAM-HAUGH.

    3 vols. Bentley. 1864.

    Le Fanu's early books had been published in Dublin. *The House by the
    Churchyard* (1863) was transferred from Dublin to London between
    printing and publication; but from the present book onward to the end
    of his life Le Fanu's novels appeared over London publishers' imprints.

10. **James, Henry.** THE PORTRAIT OF A LADY.

    3 vols. Macmillan. 1881.

    Serialized in *Macmillan's Magazine* and in *The Atlantic Monthly*. The
    English edition preceded the American by eight days.

11. **Stevenson, Robert Louis.** TREASURE ISLAND.

    Cassell. 1883.

    Serialized under the pseudonym of 'Captain George North' during
    1881/2 in *Young Folks*, to whose editor is reputed to be due the change
    from the original title, *The Sea Cook*. *Lent by Messrs. W. T. Spencer.*

12. **Kipling, Rudyard.** PLAIN TALES FROM THE HILLS.

    Calcutta: Thacker, Spink. 1888.

    This was the first collection of Kipling's short stories, most of them
    reprinted from the Lahore *Civil and Military Gazette*.

13. **Hardy, Thomas.** TESS OF THE D'URBERVILLES. THE STORY
    OF A PURE WOMAN.

    3 vols. Osgood, McIlvaine. 1891.

    Reference to the serialization of *Tess* is made in the introductory note
    to Section A.

K. *Historical and 'Period' Novels*

Here we have a mixture of quality and representativeness. *Westward
Ho!*, *The Cloister and the Hearth*, *Esmond* and *Lorna Doone* are household words, and would, for their intrinsic worth and without reference
to their being 'historical' novels, be included in any survey of nineteenth-
century fiction. On the other hand, Ainsworth, G. P. R. James and
Weyman, though competent writers if not something more, are not in
the front rank; yet they are typical 'costume-novelists', not un-
deserving of the wide popularity they enjoyed in their day. *Romola*, *The
White Company* and *Kidnapped* are here for their authors' sake, whose
fame rests on other achievements besides those here celebrated. *The
Manchester Man*, which could perhaps claim a place among the 'Dark

Horses' in Section W, is a remarkable story of Manchester between 1800 and 1830 and contains a vivid description of what was known as the 'Peterloo Massacre' of 1819. As a period piece it provokes interesting comparison with Mrs Gaskell's novels of working-class miseries in Manchester during the forties and fifties. There remains an early work (*When Charles the First Was King*) by the prolific J. S. Fletcher, whose long list of crime stories is familiar to all. It is curious to realize that as a young man he made his reputation by this romance of Cavaliers and Roundheads.

K **Ainsworth, William Harrison.** THE TOWER OF LONDON.
1. Illustrated by George Cruikshank.
Bentley. 1840.

Published in 13/12 monthly shilling parts; and in one volume, which was offered by the publishers in three styles—'handsomely bound in cloth extra, with designs by George Cruikshank on the cover, 14/6: half morocco, 17/6: and whole morocco, gilt edges, 21/-'. The copy exhibited is of the last variety and shows the Cruikshank designs. 'Publisher's leather' on the volume form of part-issued books is not often so easy to identify (most of them were in plain style), but it was commoner than has sometimes been supposed.

2. **James, G. P. R.** THE CASTLE OF EHRENSTEIN, ITS LORDS, SPIRITUAL AND TEMPORAL, ITS INHABITANTS, EARTHLY AND UNEARTHLY.
3 vols. Smith, Elder. 1847.

3. **Le Fanu, Joseph Sheridan.** THE FORTUNES OF COLONEL TORLOGH O'BRIEN. Illustrated by Phiz.
Dublin: James M'Glashan. 1847.

In the original 11/10 parts (note 'Turlogh' on covers).

4. **Thackeray, W. M.** THE HISTORY OF HENRY ESMOND, ESQ., ETC. WRITTEN BY HIMSELF.
3 vols. Smith, Elder. 1852. *Lent by Messrs Pickering & Chatto.*

5. **Kingsley, Charles.** WESTWARD HO! OR THE VOYAGES AND ADVENTURES OF SIR AMYAS LEIGH ETC.
3 vols. Cambridge: Macmillan. 1855.

This dark blue cloth became for a short time almost a 'house style' for Macmillan novels.

6. **Reade, Charles.** THE CLOISTER AND THE HEARTH, A TALE OF THE MIDDLE AGES.
4 vols. Trübner. 1861.

The original version of this story, published serially in *Once a Week* during 1859 under the title of *A Good Fight*, with illustrations by Charles Keene, was such a failure with the public that it was wound up prematurely.

3·2

7.   **'Eliot, George'.** ROMOLA.
     3 vols. Smith, Elder. 1863.

8.   **Blackmore, R. D.** LORNA DOONE. A ROMANCE OF EXMOOR.
     3 vols. Sampson Low. 1868.

9.   **Banks, Mrs Linnaeus.** THE MANCHESTER MAN.
     3 vols. Hurst & Blackett. 1876.

10.   **Stevenson, Robert Louis.** KIDNAPPED.
     Cassell. 1886.   *Lent by Messrs Pickering & Chatto.*

11.   **Doyle, A. Conan.** THE WHITE COMPANY.
     3 vols. Smith, Elder. 1891.

12.   **Fletcher, J. S.** WHEN CHARLES THE FIRST WAS KING.
     3 vols. Bentley. 1892.

13.   **Weyman, Stanley.** UNDER THE RED ROBE.
     2 vols. Methuen. 1894.   *Lent by Miss Martha Smith.*

L.   *Political Novels*

The heading to this section is used in its widest sense. It embraces a
great statesman's political philosophy (*Endymion*); a masterly example
of Trollope's genius for portraying at once the hearts of men and women
and, in detail, the social and material backgrounds to their lives—in
this case political (*Phineas Finn*); frankly propagandist fiction appealing
for co-operation between capital and labour (*Put Yourself in his Place*)
or for the amelioration of the working classes from within and not, by
legislation, from without (*Felix Holt*); a Peacockian symposium in which
such eminent persons as Jowett, Ruskin, Huxley, Matthew Arnold and
Walter Pater, under thin fictional disguise, debate every aspect of contemporary life and philosophy (*The New Republic*); Meredith's only
attempt at a political novel; Samuel Butler's famous satire on an
imaginary society; the sequel to *Marcella*, in which a rising young
politician, in Opposition, involves the heroine in what she comes to
regard, with horror and remorse, as treachery towards her husband
(*Sir George Tressady*); and a little-known specimen of the work of that
brilliant scapegrace Eustace George Grenville Murray—a novel of the
Second Empire (*The Member for Paris*).

1. **'Eliot, George'.** FELIX HOLT, THE RADICAL.
   3 vols. Edinburgh and London: Blackwood. 1866.

2. **Trollope, Anthony.** PHINEAS FINN, THE IRISH MEMBER.
   Illustrated by J. E. Millais.
   2 vols. Virtue. 1869.

3. **Reade, Charles.** PUT YOURSELF IN HIS PLACE.
   3 vols. Smith, Elder. 1870.

   No example in original cloth being available, a rebound copy is shown.
   Lent by Messrs W. T. Spencer.

4. **Murray, Eustace George Grenville.** THE MEMBER FOR PARIS.
   A TALE OF THE SECOND EMPIRE. By 'Trois Étoiles'.
   3 vols. Smith, Elder. 1871.

5. **Butler, Samuel.** EREWHON, OR OVER THE RANGE.
   Trübner. 1872.

6. **Meredith, George.** BEAUCHAMP'S CAREER.
   3 vols. Chapman & Hall. 1876.

7. **Mallock, W. H.** THE NEW REPUBLIC, OR CULTURE, FAITH
   AND PHILOSOPHY IN AN ENGLISH COUNTRY HOUSE.
   2 vols. Chatto & Windus. 1877.

8. **Disraeli, Benjamin.** ENDYMION.
   3 vols. Longmans. 1880.

9. **Ward, Mrs Humphry.** SIR GEORGE TRESSADY.
   Smith, Elder. 1896.

   (*a*) The regular published edition, in one volume.
   (*b*) Special private edition, in two volumes.

M.   *The Irish School*

This section demonstrates the individuality and vigour of the Irish school of fiction writers during the Victorian period. It was a national, not a regional, school; and, though divided within itself, it had a fundamental cohesion never achieved by either the Scottish or the Welsh novelists.

The principal cleavage between Irish novelists is between the all-Irish (nowadays acclaimed by Eire nationalism) and the Anglo-Irish. Of the former the representative *par excellence* is William Carleton, a peasant-born ultra-realist whose humour and pathos and sense of natural beauty were spontaneous and profoundly indigenous. In his wake came Mrs S. C. Hall, and Emily Lawless with her sad and sombre pictures of the Atlantic seaboard. Lever, Lover, and Maxwell are the picaresque knockabout Anglo-Irishmen, with comic 'Paddies' and slapstick dragoons and adventures abroad rather than at home. Also Anglo-Irish, but totally different in its quiet humour and sympathetic observation, is *The Real Charlotte*, by the two authors who are best known as creators of the 'Irish R.M.' Maginn, an international and tragic figure, part scholar, part gutter-journalist; Le Fanu, master of the macabre; and Marmion Savage in the semi-political, semi-satirical pages of *The Falcon Family or Young Ireland*, each present an aspect of Irishism peculiar to himself. George Moore is included as a reminder that this writer, famous for books of a very different character, was an Irishman and, when he cared to use it, had in full measure an Irishman's brooding and imaginative sense of his native land.

1. **Hall, Anna Maria.** STORIES OF THE IRISH PEASANTRY.
    Chambers. 1840.

2. **Lever, Charles.** CHARLES O'MALLEY, THE IRISH DRAGOON.
    Edited by Harry Lorrequer. Illustrated by Phiz.
    2 vols. Dublin: William Curry, Jr. 1841.
    Lent by Messrs Pickering & Chatto.

3. **Lover, Samuel.** HANDY ANDY. A TALE OF IRISH LIFE. Illustrated by the author.
    Frederick Lover and Richard Groombridge. 1842.
    Issued in parts as well as cloth.

4. **Maxwell, W. H.** THE FORTUNES OF HECTOR O'HALLARAN AND HIS MAN MARK ANTHONY O'TOOLE. Illustrated by John Leech.
    Bentley. 1842.
    The copy shown is in half calf, no example in parts or in original cloth being available.   *Lent by Mr G. G. Elliott.*

5. **Maginn, William.** JOHN MANESTY, THE LIVERPOOL MER-CHANT. Illustrated by George Cruikshank.

2 vols. John Mortimer. 1844.

6. **Savage, Marmion W.** THE FALCON FAMILY, OR YOUNG IRELAND.

Chapman & Hall. 1845.

This novel, 348 pages in one volume, bears the series imprint of *Chapman & Hall's Monthly Series*: a gallant but unsuccessful attempt to break the 31*s*. 6*d*.-for-three-volumes tradition by the issue of new fiction (as well as biography) at 7*s*. a volume, with two volumes maximum. The series expired after three years and 17 titles.

7. **Carleton, William.** THE SQUANDERS OF CASTLE SQUANDER. Plates after Topham.

2 vols. Illustrated London Library. 1852.

An example of the abortive effort to introduce silver as a rival to gold for lettering and decoration. The new technique had been exhibited by Leighton, the pioneers of publisher's cloth, at the Great Exhibition in the previous year, and it was taken up by a number of publishers in 1852 and 1853. But the silver proved sadly liable to tarnishing, so the vogue died quickly; and it was not till the eighties that a satisfactory process was finally evolved.

8. **Le Fanu, Joseph Sheridan.** THE HOUSE BY THE CHURCH-YARD.

3 vols. Tinsley. 1863.

This novel was accepted for publication by Tinsley when already printed, and some copies actually bound, in Dublin at the author's expense. Tinsley thereupon rebound the majority of bound copies in an improved style (here shown) and also reprinted title-pages. But these last, intended to supplant the Irish-printed ones, were sometimes neglected by his binder, so that various combinations occur in surviving copies. Tinsley's 'second edition' was then made up from the remaining sheets of the first, with titles again reprinted; so was the 'third edition', by now taken over by Bentley; and so, finally, was the 'remainder' (three volumes bound in one); with the result that *The House by the Church-Yard* is bibliographically one of the most complicated and confusing books of the century.

9. **Lawless, The Hon. Emily.** HURRISH. A STUDY.

2 vols. Edinburgh and London: Blackwood. 1886.

Lent by Messrs Scribners.

10. **Somerville, E. Œ., and 'Martin Ross'.** THE REAL CHAR-LOTTE.

3 vols. Ward & Downey. 1894.

11. **Moore, George.** A DRAMA IN MUSLIN.

Vizetelly. 1886.   *Lent by Richard Sadleir.*

N.   *Novels of Manners*

This double section could as easily have been a quadruple one, for in no respect were Victorian novelists more adept and prolific than in the production of *romans des mœurs*.

We lead off with Disraeli's 'Love Story' (*Henrietta Temple*), in which, for all its overwrought exaltation, burns the flame of true passion. There is good comedy among the subsidiary characters, a flattering portrait of Count d'Orsay, and sage reflections on the ways of moneylenders and the horrors of debt. *Preferment* is typical Mrs Gore—tart, racy, opulent and glittering with dubious jewellery. This copy belonged to William Beckford (who is known to have helped her in several of her books) and is annotated by him according to his practice. *Modern Flirtations* and *The Bachelor of the Albany* are self-explanatory. *Emilia Wyndham*—the frailest of stories told with surprising energy—is perhaps the most forgotten of all nineteenth-century best-sellers. It had an immense vogue and, according to its lights, deserved one. With *The Caxtons* begins the long period during which the domestic middle-class novel held sway in readers' favour. It was characteristic, alike of Bulwer Lytton's instinctive flair for what was coming, and of his inability to be himself, that he should do the right thing in the wrong way. Heralding the predominant type of mid-Victorian fiction, he must needs write a pastiche of Sterne, whereas the titles which follow (apart from poor Lady Blessington's posthumous pot-boiler), from Eden to Trollope, are all, in their several ways, straightforward expressions of their authors individualities. With Ouida's *Moths*, flamboyance flashes once more and dies, and we then find ourselves in a different world—that of the eighteen-nineties. Very typical of the last decade of the Queen's long reign are the novels shown. *Fin de siècle*, in the sense that they betray the verbal dexterities, the empty rhetoric and the wit-for-wit's sake of an exhausted epoch, they take us to the brink of a new century and of the pretentious self-indulgent vulgarities of the Edwardian carnival which recall, despite their different trappings, the 'silver fork' absurdities of seventy years earlier. As an ironic postscript is shown *Irene Iddesleigh*, which, had it been written in satire, might serve as a crazy parody of fashionable fiction both at the very beginning and the very end of our period. But Mrs Ros meant every word of it, and claims a niche of her own in the crowded panorama of Victorian novelists.

1.   **Disraeli, Benjamin.**   HENRIETTA TEMPLE.   A LOVE STORY.
     3 vols. Colburn. 1837.

2. **Gore, Mrs Catherine Francis.** PREFERMENT, OR MY UNCLE THE EARL.

3 vols. Colburn. 1840.

3. **Warren, Samuel.** TEN THOUSAND A-YEAR.

5 vols. Philadelphia: Carey & Hart. 1840/1.

Printed from the serial in *Blackwood's Magazine*, this is the first edition, preceding publication in book form in England. Until the copyright legislation of 1891 gave some protection, popular writers on each side of the Atlantic were fair game to publishers on the other, and a surprising number of well-known books first appeared on the unexpected side of the water. The subject may be studied in detail in Mr I. R. Brussel's two volumes, *Anglo-American First Editions* (Bibliographia Series, Nos. 9 and 10).

4. **Sinclair, Catherine.** MODERN FLIRTATIONS, OR A MONTH AT HARROWGATE.

3 vols. Edinburgh: William Whyte & Co. 1841.

5. **Marsh, Anne (Mrs Marsh-Caldwell)** EMILIA WYNDHAM.

3 vols. Colburn. 1846.

6. **Savage, Marmion W.** THE BACHELOR OF THE ALBANY.

Chapman & Hall. 1848.

One of the publisher's 'Monthly Series' (see note to M 6).

7. **Bulwer, Edward (Lord Lytton).** THE CAXTONS. A FAMILY PICTURE.

3 vols. Edinburgh and London: Blackwood. 1849.

8. **Blessington, Lady.** COUNTRY QUARTERS. A NOVEL. With a memoir of Lady Blessington by her neice, Miss Power. Portrait after D'Orsay.

3 vols. Schoberl. 1850.

This is Count D'Orsay's copy, specially bound for him.

9. **Eden, The Hon. Emily.** THE SEMI-DETACHED HOUSE. Edited by Lady Theresa Lewis.

Bentley. 1859.

The dark green 'bead-grain' cloth, striped with pale green, makes this a very attractive book.

10. **Meredith, George.** EVAN HARRINGTON.

3 vols. Bradbury & Evans. 1861.

The American edition, which preceded this, having been printed (by arrangement) from the serialization in *Once a Week*, bore the sub-title 'or, He would be a gentleman'.

11. **Oliphant, Margaret.** THE PERPETUAL CURATE.
     3 vols. Edinburgh and London: Blackwood. 1864.

     This is the third novel in the group known as *Chronicles of Carlingford*.

12. **Gaskell, Mrs.** WIVES AND DAUGHTERS. AN EVERYDAY
     STORY. Illustrated by George du Maurier.
     2 vols. Smith, Elder. 1866.

13. **Riddell, Mrs.** THE RACE FOR WEALTH.
     3 vols. Tinsley. 1866.

14. **Kingsley, Henry.** SILCOTE OF SILCOTES.
     3 vols. Macmillan. 1867.

15. **Wood, Mrs Henry.** GEORGE CANTERBURY'S WILL.
     3 vols. Tinsley. 1870.

     (*a*) The regular binding of claret-coloured morocco cloth.
     (*b*) Author's binding of bright blue cloth, with more ornate gilt
     decoration. Mrs Henry Wood had special bindings done (through the
     publisher and by a regular trade binder) for several of her novels, of
     which a full account is given in *More Binding Variants* by Carter and
     Sadleir (Constable, 1938).

16. **Besant, Walter, and James Rice.** READY-MONEY MORTIBOY.
     A MATTER OF FACT STORY.
     3 vols. Tinsley. 1872.

17. **Trollope, Anthony.** THE WAY WE LIVE NOW. Illustrated by
     Luke Fildes.
     2 vols. Chapman & Hall. 1875.

18. **'Ouida'** (=Louise de la Ramée). MOTHS.
     3 vols. Chatto & Windus. 1880.

     The copy shown is in a special 'presentation' or author's binding, to
     which Ouida was addicted. Isolated examples of this practice are found
     among the novels of Mrs Henry Wood, Charles Reade, Ainsworth,
     Le Fanu and others, but it was unusual in fiction publishing.

19. **Wilde, Oscar.** THE PICTURE OF DORIAN GRAY.
     Ward, Lock & Co. 1891.

     One of the 250 copies on large paper. Both this and the ordinary
     edition were designed by Charles Ricketts, and the format was, for a
     novel, as unconventional as the contents.

20. **'Hobbes, John Oliver'** (=Mrs Craigie). SOME EMOTIONS
     AND A MORAL.
     Fisher Unwin. 1891.

     Published in the *Pseudonym Library*.

21   **Benson, E. F.**   DODO. A DETAIL OF THE DAY.
2 vols. Methuen. 1892.   *Lent by John Carter.*

22.   **Corelli, Marie.**   THE SORROWS OF SATAN, OR THE STRANGE EXPERIENCE OF ONE GEOFFREY TEMPEST, MILLIONAIRE.
Methuen.. 1895.

23.   **Allen, Grant.**   THE WOMAN WHO DID.
Lane. 1895.

24.   **Cross, Victoria.**   THE WOMAN WHO DIDN'T.
Lane. 1895.

     This riposte to Grant Allen was also published in the *Keynotes Series.*

25.   **'Hope, Anthony'** (=**A. H. Hawkins**)   THE DOLLY DIALOGUES. Illustrated by Arthur Rackham.
Westminster Gazette. (1894.)

26.   **Broughton, Rhoda.**   DEAR FAUSTINA.
Bentley. 1897.

     (*a*) In the regular dark green cloth of the publisher's *Favourite Novels Series* in which the book made its first appearance.
     (*b*) In a special presentation style, being in white cloth.

27.   **Ros, Amanda McKittrick.**   IRENE IDDESLEIGH.
Belfast: W. & G. Baird. 1897.

O.   *Adventure Stories*

Although boys, according to their age, have loved—and still love—the stories here displayed, the section has purposely not been described as one (in trade parlance) of 'juveniles', because several of the books have an adult appeal also, and rank high in Victorian fiction of any category. Whereas *Masterman Ready, Coral Island, The Three Commanders* and *The Young Franc-Tireurs* are frankly boys' books, and excellent specimens of the work of famous authors who wrote them avowedly for boys, no student of the Victorian novel will dispute the right of Henry Kingsley, Rolf Boldrewood, Anthony Hope, Stevenson and Meade Falkner to an honoured place among novelists *pur sang*.

Many of these books are rarities in fine state, as our failure to provide a better *Coral Island* bears melancholy witness: one or two—notably *The Young Franc-Tireurs*—are rare in any condition.

1. **Marryat, Capt. Frederick.** MASTERMAN READY, OR THE WRECK OF THE PACIFIC. Illustrated with engravings after sketches by the author.
    3 vols. Longmans. 1841/2.

2. **Ballantyne, R. M.** THE CORAL ISLAND. A TALE OF THE PACIFIC OCEAN. Coloured plates after drawings by the author.
    Nelson. 1858.

3. **Kingsley, Henry.** RAVENSHOE.
    3 vols. Cambridge: Macmillan. 1862.

4. **Reid, Capt. Mayne.** THE HEADLESS HORSEMAN. A STRANGE TALE OF TEXAS. Illustrated with plates after Hamerton.
    Chapman & Hall, and Bentley. 1865/6.

    Published in 20 sixpenny parts, originally by Chapman & Hall but transferred to Bentley between parts XVII and XVIII; and also in 2 vols. cloth.

5. **Henty, G. A.** THE YOUNG FRANC-TIREURS, AND THEIR ADVENTURES IN THE FRANCO-PRUSSIAN WAR.
    Griffith & Farran. 1872.

    Most of Henty's previous work had been divided between conventional three-decker romances and straight war reporting. This was one of the first in the afterwards familiar pattern.

6. **Kingston, W. H. G.** THE THREE COMMANDERS. Illustrated by D. H. Friston.
    Griffith & Farran. 1876.   *Lent by Mr Arthur Rogers.*

7. **Haggard, H. Rider.** KING SOLOMON'S MINES.
    Cassell. 1885.

8. **'Boldrewood, Rolf'** (=T. A. Browne). ROBBERY UNDER ARMS: A STORY OF LIFE AND ADVENTURE IN THE BUSH AND GOLDFIELDS OF AUSTRALIA.
    3 vols. Remington. 1888.

9. **Stevenson, Robert Louis, and Lloyd Osbourne.** THE EBB-TIDE, A TRIO AND QUARTETTE.
    Heinemann. 1894.

10. **'Hope, Anthony'.** THE PRISONER OF ZENDA.
    Bristol: Arrowsmith. (1894.)
    Published in Arrowsmith's popular 'Three and sixpenny series'.

11. **Falkner, J. Meade.** MOONFLEET.
    Arnold. 1898.

P. *Social Protest*

This category could have been greatly extended, had space allowed; for the Victorian period was essentially one of awakening social conscience. Subject, however, to necessary limitations the organizers have tried to be as representative as possible, while at the same time exhibiting only novels of intrinsic literary quality or of well-reputed authorship.

The most broadly based of social protests was that which generally deplored and roundly condemned the toleration in a civilized country of a class of rich and a class of poor, between whom was so little of contact and mutual understanding as to render them two nations rather than two halves of the same nation. In the forefront of protestants of this type stands Disraeli, whose *Sybil* is actually sub-titled 'The Two Nations' and has been hailed as the original charter of Tory Democracy. The novel is at once a bitter satire on selfish aristocrats and political lick-spittles and an angry exposure of the miseries of the poor, the ameliora-tion of whose conditions of life should be—but was not—the first duty of men more fortunately placed. *Sybil* belongs to the forties; and it is interesting to read in *Demos* how the same problem presented itself in the eighties to the so different mind of George Gissing, who, sunk in his personal unhappiness, paints a bitter portrait of a demagogue, seduced by wealth and prominence into deserting the cause of the workers.

The remainder of the exhibits, though all must inevitably touch on the national tragedy of poverty and helpless suffering, have their parti-cular application. The Factory System inspires, each in its way, *John Halifax, Gentleman*, a story of 1780–1834 about the riots against the introduction of machinery and the career and heart-searchings of a self-made man; Mrs Trollope's *Michael Armstrong*, a reportage in fictional form, undertaken with the encouragement of Lord Shaftesbury, on the horrors of child-labour in factories; and Mrs Gaskell's *Mary Barton*, which, with special reference to Manchester, reveals the tragic conditions of home-life among mill-hands. Then comes a demand for Prison Reform, in *It is Never Too Late To Mend* by Charles Reade, com-bined with a vivid description of the brutalities and terrors of the Gold Rush. The evils of private madhouses, which could also have been ventilated from the bibliography of Reade, have been purposely en-trusted to William Gilbert (father of W. S. Gilbert, author of *The Bab Ballads* and the first half of Gilbert and Sullivan), whose too little-known book *Shirley Hall Asylum* would have qualified as a 'dark horse', had it not been required to do duty here.

So-called boarding schools in remote districts, which were really oubli-ettes for unwanted children (*Nicholas Nickleby*); the evils of sweating, combined with the preaching of Christian Socialism (*Alton Locke*); social hypocrisy *vis-à-vis* sexual irregularity (*The New Magdalen*) and an early manifestation of feminism and of the revolt against man-made laws and man-ruled marriages (Sarah Grand's *Heavenly Twins*) may be left to speak for themselves.

A word, however, must be said on behalf of another 'dark horse', and this time a thoroughbred. *Ginx's Baby*, by Edward Jenkins, M.P., the story of a slum baby tossed like a shuttlecock from one bumbledom to another, is one of the most remarkable short fictions of the Victorian age. It is astonishing, in view of its sensational success when it first appeared (there were 36 editions in four years), how completely it seems to be forgotten. Possibly its appearance in this exhibition may provoke a few visitors to read it for themselves. Things have, of course, changed immeasurably for the better in the sphere about which Jenkins wrote; but if one regards his little book as a comment on red tape in general, it has still an uneasy topicality.

P   **Dickens, Charles.** THE LIFE AND ADVENTURES OF NICHOLAS
1.   NICKLEBY. Illustrated by Phiz.

Chapman & Hall. 1839.

Shown here in cloth, this book was also published in 20/19 monthly parts. 48,000 were sold of the first number, which testified to the success of *Pickwick* and *Oliver Twist*.   *Lent by Messrs Charles J. Sawyer.*

2.   **Trollope, Frances.** THE LIFE AND ADVENTURES OF MICHAEL ARMSTRONG, THE FACTORY BOY. Illustrated by Hervieu, Onwhyn and Buss.

Colburn. 1839/40.

In the original 12 monthly parts.

3.   **Disraeli, Benjamin.** SYBIL, OR THE TWO NATIONS.

3 vols. Colburn. 1845.

Two copies are shown. One is in the regular half cloth, paper labels; the other is in its original folded quires, unbound. The latter shows the three labels for the binder printed together on an integral sheet of the third volume, in the position occupied in the other volumes by the half-title. This provides, by a happy chance of survival, ocular evidence of a practice quite common during the boards and boards-cloth-back period, and explains why not only *Sybil* but many other three-deckers have half-titles only in two volumes.

4.   **Gaskell, Mrs.** MARY BARTON. A TALE OF MANCHESTER LIFE.

2 vols. Chapman & Hall. 1848.   *Lent by Messrs W. T. Spencer.*

5. **Kingsley, Charles.** ALTON LOCKE, TAILOR AND POET. AN AUTOBIOGRAPHY.
   2 vols. Chapman & Hall. 1850.

6. **Sinclair, Catherine.** BEATRICE, OR THE UNKNOWN RELATIVES.
   3 vols. Bentley. 1852.

7. **Mulock, Dinah Maria (Mrs Craik).** JOHN HALIFAX, GENTLEMAN.
   3 vols. Hurst & Blackett. 1856.

8. **Reade, Charles.** IT IS NEVER TOO LATE TO MEND. A MATTER OF FACT ROMANCE.
   3 vols. Bentley. 1856.

9. **Gilbert, William.** SHIRLEY HALL ASYLUM, OR THE MEMOIRS OF A MONO-MANIAC.
   William Freeman. 1863.

10. **Jenkins, Edward, M.P.** GINX'S BABY.
    Strahan. 1870.

11. **Collins, Wilkie.** THE NEW MAGDALEN.
    2 vols. Bentley. 1873.   *Lent by Messrs Pickering & Chatto.*

12. **Gissing, George.** DEMOS. A STORY OF ENGLISH SOCIALISM.
    3 vols. Smith, Elder. 1886.   *Lent by Simon Nowell Smith.*

13. **Shaw, G. Bernard.** AN UNSOCIAL SOCIALIST.
    Swan, Sonnenschein, Lowrey & Co. 1887.

14. **'Grand, Sarah' (=Frances Elizabeth McFall).** THE HEAVENLY TWINS.
    3 vols. Heinemann. 1893.

15. **Morrison, Arthur.** TALES OF MEAN STREETS.
    Methuen. 1894.

Q. *Sport and the Open Air*

This section almost speaks for itself. Surtees, Whyte Melville and (with a smile very much their own) Somerville and Ross speak to everyone of hunting and horsemanship. Bowers, less known and (rightly) less reputed, had a keen following among hunting men of the modest kind, and is included because in the Victorian hunting-field all classes were merged in a common enthusiasm for the chase. Racing is represented by Hawley Smart and one example of the prodigious fertility of Nat Gould; boxing by *Rodney Stone*; life in the open air and the spacious country existence of the 'Old English Gentleman', by the balance of volumes shown.

1. **Mills, John.** THE OLD ENGLISH GENTLEMAN, OR THE FIELDS AND THE WOODS.
   3 vols. Colburn. 1841.

2. **Surtees, Robert Smith.** HANDLEY CROSS, OR THE SPA HUNT. A SPORTING TALE.
   3 vols. Colburn. 1843.

   In its original form *Handley Cross* was a failure. The illustrated reprint which set it on its road to fame is shown in Section F.
   Lent by Messrs Pickering & Chatto.

3. **Borrow, George.** LAVENGRO—THE SCHOLAR, THE GIPSY, THE PRIEST.
   3 vols. Murray. 1851. *Lent by Richard Jennings.*

4. **Whyte-Melville, G. J.** KATE COVENTRY. AN AUTOBIO-GRAPHY.
   John W. Parker. 1856.

   The unusual binding, of red cloth with black ink-blocked decoration, reflects the fact that Parker very rarely published fiction.
   Lent by Messrs W. T. Spencer.

5. **Jefferies, Richard.** BEVIS. THE STORY OF A BOY.
   3 vols. Sampson Low. 1882.

6. **'Wanderer'** (=E. H. D'Avigdor). A LOOSE REIN. Illustrations by G. Bowers.
   Bradbury, Agnew. 1887.

   In the original parts. Several novels by this author were so issued in the eighties, in faithful but belated imitation of Surtees.
   Lent by Messrs J. A. D. Bridger.

7. **Smart, Hawley,** LONG ODDS.
3 vols. F. V. White. 1889. *Lent by Messrs Pickering & Chatto.*

8. **Doyle, A. Conan.** RODNEY STONE. Illustrated by Sidney Paget.
Smith, Elder. 1896.

9. **Gould, Nat.** THE MAGPIE JACKET.
Routledge. 1896.

Many of Gould's sporting tales were issued alternatively in 'yellow-back'
style boards at 2*s.* and cloth at 2*s.* 6*d.*

10. **Somerville, E. Œ., and 'Martin Ross'.** SOME EXPERIENCES
OF AN IRISH R.M.
Longmans. 1899.

R. *School and University*

The organizers view with some complacence the scope and variety of
this exhibit, which runs the gamut of titles from the world-famous to
the totally unknown, yet which is throughout relevant. It is easy to
think (though far from easy to locate good copies) of *Tom Brown's
Schooldays, Eric* and *Vice Versa. Stalky and Co, Frank Fairlegh* and
Verdant Green—if only because their authors are well known—would
quickly occur to competent judges. But to track the Victorian maiden
from her select academy (*Letters Left at the Pastry-Cook's*) to a Ladies'
College (*A Girton Girl*); to share the troubles of a School Fag, the tricks
and pickings of a Scout, and the callow heartiness of *College Chums*;
to breathe the lofty atmosphere of Balliol or the varied disputatiousness
of *Liberty Hall* (how many visitors to this exhibition knew there was an
Oxford story by the author of *The Martyrdom of Man*?); these are the
reward only of arduous and fortunate search.

1. **Martineau, Harriet.** THE CROFTON BOYS.
Charles Knight. 1841.

This is the first printing, which appeared in *The Playfellow, A series of
Tales.*

2. **Hewlett, Joseph Thomas James.** PETER PRIGGINS, THE
COLLEGE SCOUT (edited by Theodore Hook, Esq.).
3 vols. Colburn. 1841.

3. **Lister, Charles.** THE COLLEGE CHUMS.
2 vols. Newby. 1845.

4. **Smedley, Frank.** FRANK FAIRLEGH, OR SCENES FROM THE LIFE OF A PRIVATE PUPIL. Illustrated by George Cruikshank.
A. Hall, Virtue & Co. 1850.

   In the original 15 monthly shilling parts (part xv, 1s. 6d.). Also published in one volume, cloth.

5. **Mayhew, Augustus.** LETTERS LEFT AT THE PASTRY-COOK'S.
Ingram, Cooke & Co. 1853.

   In addition to its interest as a very popular picture of life in a girls' school, this book is one of the earliest examples of 'yellow-back' production.

6. **'Bede, Cuthbert'** (=Edward Bradley). THE ADVENTURES OF MR VERDANT GREEN, AN OXFORD FRESHMAN.
Nathaniel Cooke. 1853.

   Together with *The Further Adventures*, etc., 1854, *Mr Verdant Green married and done for*, 1857, and *Little Mr Bouncer and his friend Verdant Green* (1873).

7. **Melly, George.** SCHOOL EXPERIENCES OF A FAG, AT A PRIVATE AND A PUBLIC SCHOOL.
Smith, Elder. 1854.

8. **Hughes, Thomas.** TOM BROWN'S SCHOOL DAYS, BY AN OLD BOY.
Cambridge: Macmillan. 1857.

   Due partly to the small number printed, partly to its great and immediate popularity and consequent hard use, and partly to the poor wearing quality of the dark blue cloth, *Tom Brown* is one of the rarest of all Victorian novels in presentable original state.

9. **Farrar, Dean F. W.** ERIC, OR LITTLE BY LITTLE.
Edinburgh: Adam & Charles Black. 1858.

10. **Reade, W. Winwood.** LIBERTY HALL, OXON.
3 vols. Charles J. Skeet. 1859.

   Written just after the author had gone down from Magdalen, this novel is dedicated to his uncle, Charles Reade.

11. **Hughes, Thomas.** TOM BROWN AT OXFORD.
3 vols. Cambridge and London: Macmillan. 1861.

   Serialized in *Macmillan's Magazine*, November 1859–July 1861, this sequel to *Tom Brown's Schooldays* was issued in 17 monthly parts in Boston and in book editions in New York (pirated) and Boston before the London edition came out.

12. **'Anstey, F.' (=T. Anstey Guthrie).** VICE VERSA, OR A LESSON TO FATHERS.
Smith, Elder. 1882.

13. **Merivale, Herman Charles.** FAUCIT OF BALLIOL.
3 vols. Chapman & Hall. 1882.

14. **Edwardes, Mrs Annie.** A GIRTON GIRL.
3 vols. Bentley. 1885.

15. **Kipling, Rudyard.** STALKY AND CO.
Macmillan. 1899.

S. *Tales of the Sea*

Virtually nothing needs to be said of this collection of sea-stories. The most famous books of the greatest of sea-novelists—Captain Marryat —are disqualified from inclusion by date of first publication, but as he continued to publish until 1850 he fully merits representation, and *The Phantom Ship* is an excellent specimen of his later manner. His 'school' is adequately on view in the persons of Edward Howard (his faithful disciple and assistant-editor on *The Metropolitan Magazine*), Chamier (his friend) and Neale (his enemy).

1. **Chamier, Capt. Frederick.** THE ARETHUSA. A NAVAL STORY.
3 vols. Bentley. 1837.

2. **Howard, The Hon. Edward Granville.** OUTWARD BOUND, OR A MERCHANT'S ADVENTURES.
3 vols. Colburn. 1838.

3. **Marryat, Capt. Frederick.** THE PHANTOM SHIP.
3 vols. Colburn. 1839.

4. **Neale, W. Johnson.** PAUL PERIWINKLE, OR THE PRESSGANG.
Illustrated by Phiz.
Tegg. 1841.   *Lent by Messrs Myers.*

5. **Kingston, W. H. G.** PETER THE WHALER, HIS EARLY LIFE AND ADVENTURES IN THE ARTIC REGIONS. Illustrated by E. Duncan.
Grant & Griffith. 1851.   *Lent by Messrs Pickering & Chatto.*

6. **Russell, W. Clark.** THE WRECK OF THE GROSVENOR.
3 vols. Sampson & Low. 1877.

7. **Pemberton, Max.** THE IRON PIRATE. A PLAIN TALE OF STRANGE HAPPENINGS AT SEA.
Cassell. 1893. *Lent by Messrs Elkin Mathews.*

8. **Jacobs, W. W.** MANY CARGOES.
Lawrence & Bullen. 1896.

9. **Kipling, Rudyard.** CAPTAINS COURAGEOUS. Illustrated by I. W. Taber.
Macmillan. 1897.

   Two copies are shown, one in its original dust-jacket. These seldom survive on books of our period, though the earliest known actually dates from the previous reign. *Lent by Major Hartley Clark.*

10. **Bullen, Frank T.** THE CRUISE OF THE CACHALOT. ROUND THE WORLD AFTER SPERM WHALES. Illustrated by A. Twidle.
Smith, Elder. 1898. *Lent by Messrs Bumpus.*

T. *Religious Themes*

Selection under this heading has been peculiarly difficult, and the results are doubtless open to severe criticism. An attempt has been made, however, to represent several types of novel concerned with religious themes or members of religious bodies, as well as contrasted specimens of the same type. Thus *Hypatia, Callista, Marius the Epicurean* and *The Sign of the Cross* deal (and how variously!) with the early stages of Christianity. *Yes and No*, violently Protestant, is a product of Christian Socialism and, as such, is relevant both to Kingsley and Newman. *Lothair* is Protestantism of another kind, demonstrating the author's conviction that in the struggle between Rome and the Anglican church the victory of the latter was essential to the 'reconstructed Tory party' as visualized by him as long ago as 1845, and therefore to the stability and survival of the British way of life. John Inglesant, the individual, is (like Lothair, the individual) a battle ground of conflicting loyalties and creeds; but the power of Shorthouse's book lies rather in its descriptive and historical passages than in the 'aliveness' or spiritual distresses of its hero. *Robert Elsmere*, on the other hand—a further story of faith beset with doubts—stands or falls by the mental agonies and minute psychological analysis of the central figure. It is hard nowadays to realize how deeply Mrs Ward's novel stirred the thoughtful public of her day. *The*

Revolution in Tanner's Lane, a classic of Dissent, stands apart from the rest, secure of survival thanks to its emotional sincerity, insight and restraint. Equally apart, though on a lower level of intellectual quality, is *The True History of Joshua Davidson*, one of the several attempts which have been made to present the life of Christ in modern dress. Three 'best-sellers' bring up the rear, which can claim to have 'religious themes' only in the sense that contemporary church conditions affect or absorb them. *The Silence of Dean Maitland* tells of an old sin with a long shadow, and on its first appearance was read by thousands with horrified delight. *The Christian*, purporting to be a philosophic exposition of the religious life of London, in fact develops into a passionate and sensuous love-story. The chief protagonists of *Red Pottage*, an enormously successful story, are of the laity, but the most effective portion of the book is the savage satire on clerical intolerance and humbug. The Rev. James Gresley is Frances Trollope's 'Vicar of Wrexhill' over again, but in terms of the late nineties and on a higher social scale.

T **Kingsley, Charles.** HYPATIA.
1. 2 vols. John W. Parker. 1853.

2. **Newman, John Henry.** CALLISTA. A SKETCH OF THE THIRD CENTURY.
Burns & Lambert. 1856.

No. XI in the 'Catholics' Popular Library'.

3. **Reynolds, The Rev. H. R., and Sir John Russell.** YES AND NO, OR GLIMPSES OF THE GREAT CONFLICT.
3 vols. Cambridge: Macmillan. 1860.

This scarce novel, written by a Congregationalist Minister and his younger brother, an eminent doctor, was never reprinted.

4. **Disraeli, Benjamin.** LOTHAIR.
3 vols. Longmans. 1870.
Presented by the author to Queen Victoria.
Lent by HIS MAJESTY THE KING.

5. **Linton, Eliza Lynn.** THE TRUE HISTORY OF JOSHUA DAVIDSON.
Strahan. 1872.

6. **Shorthouse, Joseph Henry.** JOHN INGLESANT. A ROMANCE.
Birmingham: privately printed. 1880.
Published in the following year by Macmillan, in 2 vols.

7. **Pater, Walter.** MARIUS THE EPICUREAN, HIS SENSATIONS AND IDEAS.
2 vols. Macmillan. 1885. *Lent by Richard Jennings.*

8. **'Gray, Maxwell'** (=**Miss M. G. Tuttiett**). THE SILENCE OF DEAN MAITLAND.
    3 vols. Kegan Paul, Trench & Co. 1886.

9. **'Rutherford, Mark'** (=**William Hale White**). THE REVOLUTION IN TANNER'S LANE.
    Trübner. 1887.

    Of the 1000 copies printed only the first 250 were bound in this archaistic boards-and-label style, to match the author's previous books. The remainder were later put up in conventional cloth.

10. **Ward, Mrs Humphry.** ROBERT ELSMERE.
    3 vols. Smith, Elder. 1888.

11. **Barrett, Wilson.** THE SIGN OF THE CROSS. Introduction by the Bishop of Truro.
    Macqueen. 1896.

12. **Caine, W. Hall.** THE CHRISTIAN.
    Heinemann, 1897.

    Evidence that the new novel at 6*s*. was still a trifle self-conscious is provided by the notice on the back of the title-page: '*First Edition, in One Volume, Six Shillings, consisting of* 50,000 *copies.*'

13. **Cholmondeley, Mary.** RED POTTAGE.
    Arnold. 1899.

U. *Sensation, Mystery and Crime*

Considerations of space have compressed this section, certainly as severely as—perhaps more severely than—any other. Sensation-novels of the type of *East Lynne*, *Lady Audley's Secret* and *Peg the Rake* could have been extended to make an exhibition of their own; likewise horror stories—natural and supernatural—such as those of Bulwer-Lytton, Le Fanu and Bram Stoker; likewise tales of crime, involving detection to a greater or less degree, which are here represented by the too-little-known *Paul Ferroll* and *Prince Zaleski*, and works by Wilkie Collins, Fergus Hume and Conan Doyle whose titles are household words. But such lavishness was impossible, and visitors are asked to regard this very restricted selection as a token force, behind which armies are massed in strength. Sensation, horror and crime were prolific and popular impulses to fiction during the last forty years of our period, and caused as much heart-burning among the austere as delighted engrossment among the unregenerate.

1. **Clive, Mrs Archer.** PAUL FERROLL. A TALE.
   Saunders & Otley. 1855.

2. **Bulwer, Edward (Lord Lytton).** THE HAUNTED AND THE
   HAUNTERS (in Vol. x of the First Series of *Tales from Blackwood*).
   Edinburgh: Blackwood. 1860.

   The quarterly volumes of this series collected stories which had made
   their first appearance in *Blackwood's Magazine* (see Section E).

3. **Wood, Mrs Henry.** EAST LYNNE.
   3 vols. Bentley. 1861.

4. **Braddon, Miss M. E.** LADY AUDLEY'S SECRET.
   3 vols. Tinsley. 1862.

5. **Collins, Wilkie.** THE MOONSTONE. A ROMANCE.
   3 vols. Tinsley. 1868.

6. **Le Fanu, Joseph Sheridan.** IN A GLASS DARKLY.
   3 vols. Bentley. 1872.

7. **Stevenson, Robert Louis.** DR JEKYLL AND MR HYDE.
   Longmans. 1886.

   This book was issued both in printed wrappers (as here) and in cloth.
                            Lent by Messrs Pickering & Chatto.

8. **Hume, Fergus.** THE MYSTERY OF A HANSOM CAB.
   Hansom Cab Publishing Co. (1887.)

   Originally published in Melbourne, where the first edition sold out in
   a week, this book was launched in London by an enterprising character
   named Trischler, who formed The Hansom Cab Publishing Company
   for the purpose. The earliest known surviving copy of the English
   edition carries 'Sixtieth thousand' on the title-page; the British Museum
   copy is of the 250th thouand; and though it has been suspected, perhaps
   unjustly, that Trischler's promotional zeal outran strict accuracy in
   bibliographical description, the book was certainly an immediate and
   sensational success. The copy shown here is of the 'hundredth thousand'.

9. **Doyle, A. Conan.** THE ADVENTURES and THE MEMOIRS OF
   SHERLOCK HOLMES.
   Together 2 vols. Newnes. 1892, 1894.

   Reprinted from *The Strand Magazine* with the original illustrations by
   Sidney Paget.   *Lent by Mr Arthur Rogers, Messrs William Dunlop
                            and Messrs Halewood & Son.*

10.   **'Rita'** (= **Mrs Desmond Humphries**).   PEG, THE RAKE.
3 vols. Hutchinson. 1894.

11.   **Falkner, J. Meade.**   THE LOST STRADIVARIUS.
Edinburgh and London: Blackwood. 1895.   *Lent by John Carter.*

12.   **Shiel, M. P.**   PRINCE ZALESKI.
John Lane. 1895.

No. VII of the *Keynotes Series*, cover design by Aubrey Beardsley.

13.   **Stoker, Bram.**   DRACULA.
Constable. 1897.

V.   *Some Popular Favourites*

Some of the books displayed under this heading (*The Heir of Redclyffe,
Under Two Flags, Three Men in a Boat, The Little Minister*) are
too well known to-day to require individual comment. Notes are
appended to such other titles as, in their time, had a great vogue but
are now titles and sometimes little more.

1.   **Taylor, Captain Meadows.**   CONFESSIONS OF A THUG.
3 vols. Bentley. 1839.

This sensational—indeed gruesome—story of murder and violence in
India was written by a man intimately familiar with native life and
character. But for his military duties, Meadows Taylor would probably
have become Commissioner for the Suppression of Thuggee and
Dacoity, a post given to Sir William Sleeman in February 1839. The
'Confessions' are genuine, being those of a Thug who confessed to
seven hundred murders, and the entire novel is based on the author's
personal observation and experience. The curious are recommended to
Taylor's admirable autobiography, *The Story of My Life* (1877).

2.   **Cobbold, Richard.**   THE HISTORY OF MARGARET CATCH-
POLE, A SUFFOLK GIRL.   Illustrated by the author.
3 vols. Colburn. 1845.

An example of that rare phenomenon, a three-decker with illustrations.
    Another romance founded on fact, presenting the true experiences of
a girl living near Ipswich who had been befriended by Cobbold's father.
As a record of smuggling on the Suffolk coast and of the adventurous
lives of country and fisher folk in the early years of the century *Margaret
Catchpole* is a document of permanent value. The Rev. Richard Cobbold,
a sporting parson and indefatigable amateur artist as well as a writer,
was a member of a famous and wealthy East Anglian family.

3.   **Yonge, Charlotte M.**   THE HEIR OF REDCLYFFE.
2 vols. John W. Parker. 1853.

4. **'Ouida'.** UNDER TWO FLAGS
    3 vols. Chapman & Hall. 1867.

5. **Mathers, Helen.** COMIN' THRO' THE RYE.
    3 vols. Bentley. 1875.

    The author's first and most successful novel.
    One of the best loved of Victorian sentimental romances, telling with
    somewhat affected grace and tenderness of the pleasant lives and suitable
    amours of young people of the upper middle-class. It appeared
    anonymously, but its immediate success brought Helen Mathers' name
    to the title-pages of her second and little less popular full-length novel
    Cherry Ripe. The story is told in the first person and the present tense,
    which conventions, operating jointly throughout three volumes, tend to
    become tiresome. Miss Mathers' success greatly annoyed Rhoda
    Broughton, who in her letters to the embarrassed George Bentley (after
    all, the Mathers was also a Bentley author and a very profitable one)
    sneered continually at her rival's saccharine flimsiness.

6. **Fothergill, Jessie.** THE FIRST VIOLIN.
    3 vols. Bentley. 1878.

    This is the first published edition.
    A musical novel staged in Düsseldorf ('Elberthal') and told in two
    first person narratives. 'Music and cotton-mills' were declared by a
    contemporary critic to be Miss Fothergill's chief inspirations, and in
    this work the former is dominant. The novel had a very large sale, and
    to some degree forecast two comparatively recent and also successful
    books, *Maurice Guest* and *Martin Schüler*. If, like that remarkable
    musical novel *Charles Auchester* (1853), it is a *roman à clé*, no clue, to
    our knowledge, survives to any fictional portrayal of real persons.

7. **Jerome, Jerome K.** THREE MEN IN A BOAT (TO SAY NOTHING
    OF THE DOG).
    Bristol: Arrowsmith. 1889.

8. **Barrie, J. M.** THE LITTLE MINISTER.
    3 vols. Cassell. 1891.

9. **Harraden, Beatrice.** SHIPS THAT PASS IN THE NIGHT.
    Lawrence & Bullen. 1893.

    To one reader, at least, the popular success of this short novel is in-
    explicable. It has certain excellent qualities—natural, deftly varied
    dialogue, passages of acute, if sometimes bitter, observation, and a
    sincerity which goes some way to redeem a general tendency to over-
    solemnity. But there is a fatal strain of whimsy, an almost Bulwerian
    high-falutin ('the road to High Ideals leading the Traveller to the Temple
    of True Knowledge') and a general air of rhapsodical unreality, which,
    one would have thought, could be relied on to bore all but the loftiest
    highbrows. Yet the book triumphed, and Miss Harraden with it.

10.   Du Maurier, George. TRILBY. Illustrated by the author.

3 vols. Osgood, McIlvaine. 1894.

When *Trilby* was originally serialized in *Harper's Magazine*, objection was taken to the marked resemblance between the illustration of Joe Sibley and the tolerably well-known features of Whistler. In the book, Sibley was given a beard. The magazine is here shown alongside.

11.   Zangwill, Israel. CHILDREN OF THE GHETTO. A STUDY OF A PECULIAR PEOPLE.

3 vols. Heinemann. 1894.

The novel which made Zangwill's reputation cannot be better acclaimed than by quoting from Alfred Sutro's article in the *D.N.B.* 'It gave the real Jew to the world, revealing him as he had never been revealed before, minimizing nothing, extenuating nothing, exaggerating nothing, handling him with profound knowledge and with affection, but also with justice.'

12.   Steele, Flora Annie. ON THE FACE OF THE WATERS. Heinemann. 1896.

W.   *Some Dark Horses*

In the previous section due obeisance was paid to a representative, but miscellaneous, group of books which were all great favourites in their day, and some of which still are. In this final section the organizers have indulged themselves by picking out a dozen books all of which are generally neglected to-day, most of which were neglected by their contemporaries, but each of which we believe to have quality and to deserve rescue from oblivion.

We offer this selection for the Parnassus Handicap in the happy confidence that rival tipsters will be infuriated where they agree and contemptuous where they do not. But publishers of reprint series are hereby invited to help themselves without charge.

1.   Gore, Mrs. CECIL, OR THE ADVENTURES OF A COXCOMB.

3 vols. Bentley. 1841.

This novel is exceedingly rare in original state, and a bound copy is shown here.

One of the swiftest and wittiest of Mrs Gore's many novels of smart Society life, *Cecil* describes the rise to social proficiency of a *flâneur* of outstanding gifts. Amused by the foibles of his kind, yet determined to become a leader of the 'ton', Cecil, in first person memoir form, tells his tale and airs his views on life.

The period is the first quarter of the century; and Cecil, as a Member of Parliament, travelling 'Milord', as an intimate friend of Byron in Italy, and as a 'wit among lords' and a 'lord among wits', shows us through disillusioned but complacent eyes the panorama of the smart world of the day. A sequel, *Cecil a Peer*, carries the story from 1830. It may be noted that *Cecil*, when reissued in one-volume form, was re-entitled *Ormington*.

2.   **'Barrowcliffe, A. J.' (= Alfred Mott).** NORMANTON. Smith, Elder. 1862.

Traditional enough in plot (stern father, erring daughters, ultimate violent death of wicked seducer), this short novel is told with a delicacy, with a sense of landscape and of seasonal characteristics, with a tenderness towards animals and weak things generally, and with a mastery of prose-rhythm, which put Barrowcliffe as a literary artist in the front rank of Victorian novelists. He wrote, in addition to *Normanton*, one three- and one two-decker. His books are extremely rare and nothing is said of him in works of reference. His real name was Alfred Mott.

3.   **Marsh, Anne (Mrs Marsh-Caldwell).** CHRONICLES OF DART-MOOR. 3 vols. Hurst & Blackett. 1866.

Mrs Marsh-Caldwell is already represented in Section N by her most popular novel *Emilia Wyndham*. In *Chronicles of Dartmoor* we have a work of greater literary significance, though of much smaller contemporary fame. Staged in a village lost in the heart of the moor, it portrays an almost barbaric way of life, led by a tiny community untouched by modern influences. Superstition and age-old custom dominate the place, and the *Cambridge History of English Literature* finds in the book 'a remarkable anticipation of one aspect of the Wessex novels'.

4.   **Riddell, Mrs.** FAIRY WATER 1873, THE UNINHABITED HOUSE 1875, THE HAUNTED RIVER 1877, THE DISAPPEARANCE OF JEREMIAH REDWORTH 1878. Routledge Christmas Annuals.

For the sake of their outward appearance, on account of their extreme rarity in unmutilated form, and because they show the author's talent for the macabre and the ghostly at its best, these four novelettes are displayed in series. A publisher has announced a 'revival reprint' of Mrs Riddell's *Weird Stories*, and here is material for a similar venture. All four are ghost stories, the first laid in Essex, the other three at Addlestone in the marshy expanse of the Thames Valley, where the river, a disused canal, and the stream which once fed a rotting mill whisper behind the sinister curtain of wintry fog.

5.   **Baring Gould, S.** MEHALAH. A STORY OF THE SALT MARSHES. 2 vols. Smith, Elder. 1880.

A truly powerful, if melodramatic, story of peasant folk in the Essex salt marshes. The heroine, Mehalah, is a passionate girl of gipsy origin

5 (*continued*)

who is tricked into marriage by a malignant and ruthless villian called Rebow. In revenge she blinds him with vitriol, and the ill-starred union drags through a few savage weeks until the man, having stunned the woman, chains her to himself and deliberately drowns the pair of them. The rustic folk among whom Mehalah lives are portrayed with sympathy and humour, and the sensational plot is skilfully handled by a born story-teller.

6.   Oliphant, Margaret. A BELEAGUERED CITY.

Macmillan. 1880.

A short novel, told in a series of personal narratives, describing strange happenings in the little Burgundian town of Sémur. The dead rise from their graves, mass in an invisible crowd outside the walls and close down on the town like a cloud of ice-cold darkness. The people flee for refuge to the surrounding countryside, while Sémur remains shrouded in sombre fog. For three days the place is 'possessed', until the spirits are exorcized (or laid to rest) by the courage of the Mayor and the Curé, who penetrate the haunted and deserted town and celebrate Mass in the empty Cathedral.

7.   Woods, Margaret L. A VILLAGE TRAGEDY.

Bentley. 1887.

This first novel by the wife of the President of Trinity College Oxford (later Master of the Temple) is based on an incident which occurred in the village of Garsington. It is a short, grim, well-proportioned tale of a girl cruelly treated by an uncle and aunt, who takes refuge with her cowherd lover. On the eve of their wedding the man is killed by a train, and Annie is left to bear loneliness, poverty and a pregnancy shunned by the neighbours because without benefit of clergy. The end is tragedy.

Mrs Woods, who lived until 1945, was born a Bradley and, both in Oxford and the Temple, played hostess with much distinction. She was a gifted poet, and her work, whether in poetry or prose, blended sensitive melancholy with a realism almost harsh in its directness.

8.   Pryce, Richard. JUST IMPEDIMENT.

Ward & Downey. 1890.

Pryce, like Merrick (see no. 12), was insufficiently appreciated. As scrupulous an artist, he failed even more sadly to achieve popularity— in his own country that is, for in America two of his later books, *Christopher* and *David Penstephen*, made their mark. But whereas Merrick wrote with nonchalant gaiety about the fringes of literary Bohemia, Pryce had his share of the sombre dramatic sense of his native Wales and painted his pictures of polite society with fearless logic. *Just Impediment* (although an early book) has been selected for the sake of its unusual and rather courageous plot and for the many admirable glimpses it provides of the London townscape and the social manners of the period.

9. **Cholmondeley, Mary.** DIANA TEMPEST.
3 vols. Bentley. 1893.

An extremely well written and shrewdly characterized story of a feckless conceited man who sees an expected inheritance pass to his nephew. In his fury he makes a compact with a murderous rogue who instigates a series of plots to remove the unwanted boy. Side by side with this sensational tale go the love affair of Diana Tempest, daughter of the disinherited man, and gaily satirical descriptions of social events and social types. Altogether a remarkable production for a clergyman's daughter in her early thirties, showing a sense of character and a wisdom as to human nature which contributed largely to the triumph, six years later, of her best known novel *Red Pottage* (see Section T).

10. **Coleridge, Mary E.** THE SEVEN SLEEPERS OF EPHESUS.
Chatto & Windus. 1893.

George Meredith is reputed to have said that if this novel had been completed it would have ranked with the most remarkable of the century. Even unfinished, it is a highly original and effective affair.
Lent by John Carter.

11. **'Merriman, Henry Seton'** (= H. S. Scott). THE SOWERS.
Smith, Elder. 1896.

Merriman's plots, characters and situations make his neglect by Hollywood a mystery, and his dialogue and worldly-wise reflections are a constant joy to the amateur of period flavour. He initiated the cult of the 'strong, silent man', and *The Sowers* actually has two of them.
Lent by John Carter.

12. **Merrick, Leonard.** CYNTHIA, A DAUGHTER OF THE PHILIS-TINES.
Chatto & Windus. 1896.

This was Merrick's fifth book of fiction, yet the first to display what became the dominant characteristics of his later work. He was an admirable example of what are called 'Authors' Authors'—that is to say, his style, delicacy of touch and literary integrity endeared him to fellow craftsmen, but from the general public he never had the welcome the quality of his work deserved. *Cynthia* is the story of a marriage between the writer of one highly praised but not very successful novel and the daughter of a stockbroker. It begins lightly and wittily in France, continues in England through the subtle stages of mutual misunderstanding and ends on a pretty note of sentiment. Publishers, editors, contracts and book-reviews play a large part in the tale, which, like so many of its successors, was too nearly the French *conte* and not sufficiently the solid English novel to please the bulk of library subscribers. Maurice Hewlett, in a preface to a new edition of the novel, wrote: 'Cynthia is one of Mr Merrick's loveliest women; and he has made many lovely women.'

13. **Harland, Henry.** THE CARDINAL'S SNUFF BOX.

Lane. 1900.

Born in Russia of American parents, Harland went through Harvard and
became a city official in New York. He wrote several sensational books,
mostly of Jewish interest, under the name of Sidney Luska; but in 1890
he suddenly migrated to London, where he became an expatriate
æsthete and the first editor of *The Yellow Book*. *The Cardinal's Snuffbox*
was the third work of fiction of his European sojourn and was widely
and deservedly popular. Staged among the fertile beauties of inland
Lombardy, this love-story of an English novelist and an Italian duchess
has the heady charm and perfumed sentiment proper to a romantic
episode played out in those carefree days under Italian skies.

INDEX OF AUTHORS

Index of Authors

Plate 1. These and many other magazines carried serialised fiction (see Section A)

Plate II. The part-issue and its cloth volume in the early decorated style (see K3)

Plate III. A later part-issue, with its two-volume book edition
in the plainer style (see B4)

Plate IV. The severe boards-and-label style,
inlierited from the Regency (see C1)

Plate V. Alternative styles : half-cloth with labels and full cloth lettered in gilt (see C2)

Plate VI. Full cloth, gilt, was the rule by the sixties (see M8)

Plate VII. A typical, rather ugly, product
of the seventies (see L6)

Plate VIII. An uncompromisingly plain
example from the eighties (see J10)

Plate IX. Bentley enlivens the last days of the
three-decker with lavish decoration (see C7)

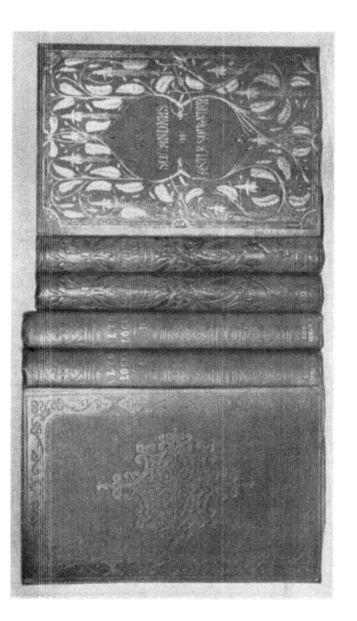

Plate X. A plain and a fancy example of the mid-century two-decker (see P5 and M7)

Plate XI. One-volume novels, early and late (see N9 and N22)

Plate XII. A selection of volumes from the cloth-bound fiction series described in Section E

Plate XIII. Examples of boarded fiction series (see Section E), including some yellow-backs

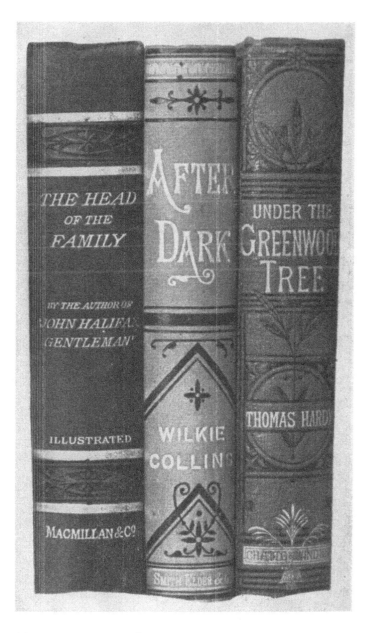

Plate XIV. A trio of one-volume reprints from Section D.

Plate XV. Trollope's Lady Dumbello and Mr. Palliser, by J. E. Millais

Plate XVI. Macmillan's *Cranford* and *Illustrated Standard Novels* series (see F10 and F11)

Printed in the United States
By Bookmasters